بسم الله الرحمن الرحيم

ISBN 978-0-9563568-1-9

First Edition, 2011

HSBT Publications

17-19 Ombersley Road, Balsall Heath, Birmingham, B12 9UR

Questions and suggestions welcomed at:

atherhussain@hotmail.com

Design, printed & bound in the UK by OUTSTANDING

TOWARDS UNDERSTANDING AQIDAH

Hafiz Ather Hussain al-Azhari

HSBT Publications

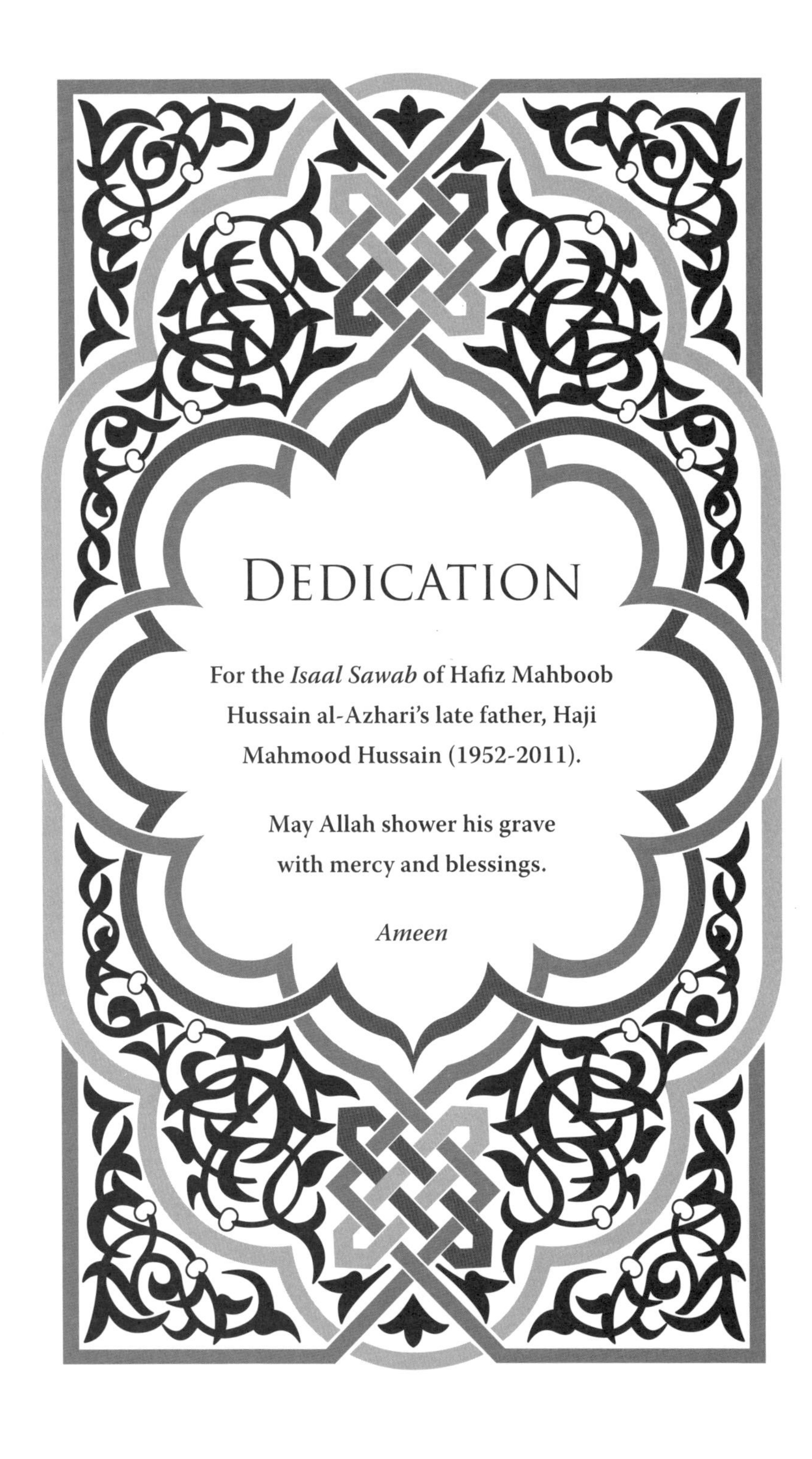

Dedication

For the *Isaal Sawab* of Hafiz Mahboob Hussain al-Azhari's late father, Haji Mahmood Hussain (1952-2011).

May Allah shower his grave with mercy and blessings.

Ameen

Contents

Foreword

Towards Understanding Aqidah is the recent academic work of Moulana Hafiz Ather Hussain al-Azhari. As the name indicates, in this book he has outlined in a scholarly way the fundamentals of Islam. He has taken great care in consulting references in order to dispel some of the misinterpretations of Islam. The contents and its presentation are clearly outstanding and his approach is very focused. He has devoted a great deal of his energy in the collection of information he includes in this work. In my opinion this is a very good example of an inspiring initiative.

In the present theological climate of the Muslim world many young people ask 'Where do we go to understand Islam?' Going to a mosque or Islamic institution only may provide an incomplete understanding of this great religion because the code of conduct of our centres are perceived by so many of us as biased and partial. Consequently we must go to the scholarship and authentic sources of Islam to acquire a broad and accurate insight. I believe that this book fulfils this criterion and will be immensely helpful in providing guidance to the original and organic teachings of Islam.

It is an irony that sources and avenues of Islamic literature and its dispensation on a large scale has also led to an internal misunderstanding of Islam in our age. Accordingly we are experiencing a climate of intolerance and fear, resulting in an undercurrent of repulsion and frustration within a section of young Muslims.

I am pleased that this book is being published at a time when such independent and neutral analysis of our theological resources is greatly required and I pray to Allah Almighty that readers find it a straightforward reading on the topic of Aqidah and benefit from it, Ameen.

Finally I congratulate Moulana Ather Hussain al-Azhari for his efforts and hope that this work will be widely appreciated by all.

Moulana Mohammad Shahid Raza Na'imi,

Head Imam, Leicester Central Mosque.

22 January 2011.

Preface

Towards Understanding Aqidah is a short introduction to the basic beliefs that each and every Muslim is required to believe in. In essence, the Aqidah of the Ahl Sunna in this book will be based on *Īmān Mufassal* which all Muslims learn from a young age:

امنت باالله و ملائكته و كتبه و رسله و اليوم الاخر و
القدر خيره و شره من الله تعالي و البعث بعد الموت

'I believe in Allāh, and His angels, and His scriptures, and His Messengers, and the Last Day, and in destiny; the good and bad of it is from Allāh and [I believe] in resurrection after death.'

This itself is derived directly from the famous *Hadīth of Jibrā'īl*, in which the Prophet ﷺ defined Faith (Īmān) as:

> '[That] you believe in Allāh, His angels, His scriptures, His Messengers, the Last Day, and that you believe in *Qadr*, the good and bad of it.' [1]

---

1 *Sahīh Muslim*, Book of Faith, Hadīth no. 9.

In this book, each aspect of our belief has been explained in separate chapters. For the sake of clarity, each chapter has then been divided into easily-understandable sub-sections. Owing to its importance, the work concludes with a chapter devoted to Bid'a.

Many Muslims in this day and age are confused about their Aqidah and are unsure what they are required to believe in. To give content to the reader, the book has relied on explaining our Aqidah using the earliest sources possible. Great care has been taken to reference each verse, Hadith and opinion to its primary source. A detailed bibliography has also been provided at the end of the book.

The book in front of you is thanks to the effort of several people, to whom I am eternally indebted. Firstly, I sincerely thank my family in general and my parents in particular, who have been a constant source of love, comfort and inspiration. Secondly, I express gratitude to all of my teachers, especially Moulana Abdul Bari Sahib and M.I.H. Pirzada Sahib. Thirdly, I am thankful to the staff behind Hazrat Sultan Bahu Trust (Birmingham) and the Islamic Centre (Leicester), who have provided me with a brilliant platform to propagate Islam. Hazrat Allama Pir Nayaz al-Hasan Qadiri Sahib is particularly worthy of praise and thanks, for his love and advice. Finally, I am grateful to Allama Mohammad Shahid Raza Na'imi, who is the inspiration behind this book. In the summer of 2009, he approached me and Mufti Muhammad Shakir Misbahi, requesting us to design and deliver a course on the Aqidah of the Ahl al-Sunna, at Leicester Central Mosque. Hundreds of Muslim men and women attended the course over a ten-week period during the Autumn of that year. This book is based on the notes recorded during this course. Allama Shahid Raza Sahib's piety, wisdom and knowledge continues to astound me as each day passes.

Though a full transliteration has not been offered for the Arabic words, a basic form has been provided to create ease for the reader. The letter

Waw (preceded by a *Dhamma*) is represented by 'ū' (as in Sūrah), the letter *Alif* (preceded by a *Fatha*) with 'ā' (as in Fātiha) and the letter *Ya* (preceded by a *Kasra*) with 'ī' (as in Hadīth).

The commendable parts of this work are due to Allah's limitless favour and mercy. The shortcomings are all my own.

Finally, I request the readers to remember me in their Dua's. May Allah forgive our sins and grant us Paradise in the hereafter- Ameen.

Ather Hussain al-Azhari.

BA Principles of Theology, Al-Azhar University, Cairo,
MPhil Theology & BA Political Science, University of Birmingham,
MA Arabic & Islamic Studies, Bhera Sharif, Pakistan.

Introduction

a. What is Aqīdah?

'Aqīdah (عقيدة) derives from the root word *Aqada* in Arabic, which means 'to tie and bind something'.[1] When a person forms a contract or agreement with someone, then the Arabs call this an *Aqd*. This is because by agreeing to something, they are 'binding' their ties. The marriage ceremony is referred to as *Aqd Nikāh* by Arabs, because it is an agreement between the couple that ties their relationship.

In Islamic terms, *Aqīdah* refers to the doctrines that each and every Muslim is tied to. It refers to the beliefs that he/she agrees to adhere to as a believer.

b. What areas does Aqīdah cover?

In short, it is possible to identify three broad areas that this discipline covers;

i. al-Ilāhīyyāt; namely everything that is related to our belief in God.

1 See *Lisān al-Arab* (vol. IX, p. 309). Ibn Manzūr (d.711/1311).

ii. al-Nabūwwāt; this refers to all matters related to the prophets and messengers.

iii. al-Sam'īyyāt; this refers to those matters relating to our Aqīdah that we could never understand and comprehend except from a heard source, namely Allāh and His Prophet ﷺ. For instance, our Aqīdah requires that we believe in punishment and reward in the grave. The only way we know this is because we heard it from the Qur'ān and Sunna. Likewise, our belief in the questioning (in the grave and on the Day of Judgement), in Paradise and in Hell are all considered as al-Sam'īyyāt.

c. Why is Aqīdah important?

In short, the acceptance of our actions is dependant on our faith, or Aqīdah. All our worships are only accepted when it is coupled with the correct belief.

For example, people are described in the Qur'ān who perform Salāh but are still subject to Allāh's dismay (107: 4-7) and who build mosques but still lack piety (9: 107-8). This is because they had the wrong Aqīdah. Repeatedly in the Qur'ān, Allāh gives glad-tiding to those 'who believe *and* perform good actions.' In other words, the right doctrine is the basis for the acceptance of our actions.[2]

---

2 We find that in one famous report, the Prophet ﷺ said: 'Islām is built upon five [pillars]; the testimony that there is no God but Allāh and that Muhammad is the Messenger of Allāh, to establish prayer, to give Zakāh, Hajj and to fast in Ramadān (*Sahih al-Bukhārī*; Book of Faith, Hadīth no.7). Some reports exist in which the Prophet (peace and blessings of Allāh be upon him) mentioned 'fasting in Ramadān' before 'Hajj' (*Sahīh Muslim*, Book of Faith, Hadīth no. 19). But all the variations of this Hadīth commence with the testimony that there is no God but Allāh and that Muhammad is the Messenger of Allāh. This too implicitly implies that faith (the testimony) always precedes actions (Hajj, Salāh, Zakāh and Sawm).

d. The Aqīdah of the Ahl Sunna; its source.

Our Aqīdah is derived directly from the Qur'ān and Sunna of the Prophet ﷺ. The task to formulate and explain it has been left to the scholars, like the four great Imāms (namely Imām Abū Hanīfa (d. 150/767), Imām Shāfi'ī (d. 204/819), Imām Mālik (d. 179/795) and Imām Ahmad ibn Hanbal (d. 241/855)), Imām al-Tahāwī (d. 321 A.H./933 C.E.), Abū al-Hasan al-Ash'arī (d. 324/936) and Abū Mansūr al-Māturīdī (d. 333/944).

Chapter One

Belief in Allāh

1.0. Īmān and Islām.

• Īmān.

هو تصديق بالقلب

Īmān means to believe and verify with the heart. In other words, to accept whatever the Prophet ﷺ brought.[3]

• Islām.

هو الاقرار باللسان بالشهادتين مع التصديق بالقلب

Islām means the verbal affirmation of the two testimonies (that there is none worthy of worship except Allāh and that Muhammad is the Last Messenger), along with believing this with the heart.[4]

Islām consists of five pillars (i) to testify that there is none worthy of worship except Allāh and that Muhammad is the Last Messenger (ii) to

3 p. 28. *Sharh al-Risāla al-Nāfi'a wa al-Hujaj al-Qāti'a*. Sheikh Muhammad Abd al-Latīf Sālih al-Farfūr (d. 1407/1986).

4 Ibid.

establish Prayer (iii) to give Zakāh (iv) to fast in Ramadān (v) to perform Hajj.[5]

If a person denies the legitimacy of one of these five pillars, then he becomes a non-believer, Islamic Sharī'ah is no longer applicable to him and he will not be buried in a Muslim cemetery.

1.1. What is *Tawhīd*?

In the Arabic language, this word stems from the word for 'one', because this is the main attribute of Allāh, His Oneness. In Islamic terminology, *Tawhīd* is a branch of knowledge from which we are able to understand the oneness of Allāh - in essence, attributes and actions.

In short, this field of knowledge refers to Allāh Almighty and helps us to identify:

1. What is necessary for Him. For example, Allāh has and will always exist.
2. What is permissible for Him. For example, Allāh can create and destroy.
3. What is impossible for Him. In short, these are all attributes of imperfection.

---

5 This definition of Īmān and Islām is taken from the Prophet's own explanation in the *Hadīth* of *Jibrīl*. Jibrīl appeared in the presence of the Prophet ﷺ and asked: 'O Muhammad! Inform me about Islām.' The Prophet ﷺ replied: 'That you testify that there is no God except Allāh, and that Muhammad is the Messenger of Allāh, and that you establish Prayer, that you give Zakāh, that you fast in Ramadān and that you perform the Hajj if you are able to do so.' Jibrīl then asked about Īmān to which the Prophet ﷺ replied: '[That] you believe in Allāh, His angels, His scriptures, His Messengers, the Last Day, and that you believe in *Qadr*, the good and bad of it.' (*Sahīh Muslim*, Book of Faith, Hadīth no.9).

1.2. The Attributes of Allāh.

The scholars have divided the attributes of Allāh into many different types.[6] For the sake of clarity, the main attributes of Allāh are listed below with a brief description.

i. *al-Qidm* (pre-existent). In other words, His existence cannot be ascribed to a particular time and it does not have a beginning. When we say that Allāh is *Qadīm*, it means He has no beginning. Allāh existed before anything else did and He has always existed. In the Qur'ān, Allāh is described as:

> 'He is the First (nothing is before Him) and the Last (nothing is after Him).' (57:3)

Hence, there is a difference between our existence (and everything in the universe) and Allāh's existence. The *Wujūd* (existence) of Allāh is pre-eternal and ever-lasting and He did not require someone to bring Him into existence. Allāh existed when nothing else did.

As for our existence, it is *Hādith* (حادث), meaning it is dependant on a creator and on time and place. Our existence – unlike Allāh's – does have a beginning and end.

ii. *al-Baqā* (ever-living). In other words, He is not subject to death or decay. When we say that Allāh is *Bāqi*, it means He will never have an end. The Qur'ān states:

> 'Whoever is on it (the earth) will perish. And the Face of your Lord full of majesty and honour will abide forever' (55: 26-27).

iii. *al-Mukhālafa li al-Hawādith* (contrary to created things). Allāh

---

6 *Sifa Nafsiyya*, *Sifa Salbiyya*, *Sifa Maʻānī* and *Sifa Maʻnawiyya*.

does not resemble anyone or anything from His creations, not in essence, attributes or actions. The Qur'ān affirms that 'there is nothing like Him' (42: 11).

A pious man from our ancestors saw the Prophet ﷺ in his dream. He asked him: 'What is the essence of *Tawhīd*?' The Prophet ﷺ replied: 'Whatever you think Allāh is like, He is different to that.'[7]

iv. *al-Wahdāniyya* (oneness). In other words, He is not subject to division and numbers, as clarified perfectly in Sūrah Ikhlās.

v. *al-Qiyām bi al-Nafs* (self-supportive). This means that Allāh is not dependant upon anyone or anything for His continued existence. He is free from all types of support. Rather, the entire universe is dependant on Him.

vi. *Wājib al-Wujūd* (necessary existence). Everything in this world that we see did not exist at one point in time. For example, the sun at one point in time did not exist. There must have been a force or creator which brought the sun into existence. This creator itself must have always existed and must not have depended on anything else for its own existence. This is Allāh and He is what we term *Wājib al-Wujūd*; that His ever-existence is compulsory.

Additionally, the scholars outline that Allāh Almighty is:

vii. All-Able.

viii. Does what He intends.

ix. All-Knowing.

---

7 p. 39. *Sharh al-Risāla al-Nāfi'a wa al-Hujaj al-Qāti'a*. Sheikh Muhammad Abd al-Latīf Sālih al-Farfūr (d. 1407/1986).

x. All-Listening.[8]

xi. All-Seeing.

xii. Capable of dialogue.

xiii. Alive.

1.3. What attributes cannot be associated with Allāh Almighty?

- The opposite of the aforementioned attributes are impossible for Allāh Almighty. For example, Allāh is *Bāqī* and so it is impossible for Him to be *Fānī* (subject to perish).

- It is astonishing to hear the Fatwa of Sheikh Rashīd Ahmad Gangūhī[9], the first Sheikh al-Hadīth of Dār al-Ulūm Deoband, in *Fatāwa Rashīdiyya*, in which he suggests that it is possible for Allāh to lie. He writes:

> 'The meaning of the possibility of Allāh lying is that it is within the power of Allāh to lie, meaning that whatever punishment has been promised (for the sinners) by Allāh, He has the power to do the opposite of that even if He does not do it....so the belief of all the scholars, Sufis and Ulama of Islām is that lies are within the power of Allāh.'[10]

---

8 When we see and hear, then this is dependant on other factors and instruments. If our eyes are covered then this affects our ability to see. If the sound is too low, then we cannot hear. However, Allāh's seeing and listening is free from such factors. He does not require eyes and ears to see and hear and more importantly, nothing can escape His senses (p. 51, *al-Aqīda al-Hasana (al-Mar'ūf bi) Aqā'id al-Islām*. Hazrat Shāh Walī Allāh Muhaddith Delhvī.

9 An Indian scholar who lived in the late 19th and early 20th century. He was the co-founder of Dār al-Ulūm Deoband in India, which resulted in the school of thought popularly known as Deobandism.

10 *Fatāwa Rashīdiyya*. Sheikh Rashīd Ahmad Gangūhī. Vol. I, p. 20, Lines 11-15. Kutub

This clearly contravenes the Qur'ān which asserts that:

- 'Surely Allāh never fails in His promise.' (3:9)

- 'Who is more true in statement than Allāh?' (4: 87)

Moreover, one of Allāh's beautiful names is *Haqq* (the Truth).

The mainstream Sunni scholars do hold the belief that Allāh can do what He wishes, but Sheikh Rashīd Ahmad has confused Muslims by scandalously terming this as 'Imkān al-Kazib', or 'the possibility of lying'. Sheikh Jibrīl Haddād writes:

> 'It is astonishing that the Deobandī Sheikhs showed such eloquence and righteous care in refusing to attribute the Prophet ﷺ the attribute *Ālim al-Ghaib* (knower of the unseen), lest it suggest *Shirk*...yet when it comes to the Divine Attributes, the Deobandī Shuyūkh come up with a new term [Imkān al-Kazib] which not only has no verbatim textual stipulation either – 'Imkān al-Kazib' – but also contradicts the Divine Attribute of *Sidq* (Truth) in the Qur'an!' [11]

In short, we believe that Allāh possesses all attributes of perfection and

---

Khāna Rahīmiyya, Delhi, India.

11 Sheikh Jibrīl Haddād adds:
'In addition, Ashraf Alī Thānwī (d. 1362/1943) is also accused of attributing Allāh Most High the "power to lie" in translating the meaning of the verse {*wa makarū wa makara Allāh wallāhu khayru al-mākirīn*, 3:54} - "They schemed and Allāh schemed, and Allāh is the best of schemers" to read "They 'makkarbaaz' [which in Urdu connotes cunning and other despicable attributes unbefitting to Allāh], He 'makkarbaaz', and He is the best of those who makkarbaaz." But the latter accusation is groundless, as Allāh Himself attributes to Himself the Arabic verb makara in His Book, and to deny such attribution or decry it is impermissible. However, it is equally impermissible to understand or explain it in terms of the *Makr* of creatures. The authorities said that verses such as {They schemed, and Allāh schemed, and Allāh is the best of schemer} are based on mushakala, i.e. a figure of speech whereby Allāh attributes to Himself the same word as He applies to the wrongdoers' act but in a different sense, which they explained to mean: "He throws back upon them [the fruits of] their own scheming."' (www.livingislam.org)

beauty and therefore all traits of imperfection are impossible for Him, such as lying, deceit and oppression.[12] Knowing that Allāh is able to do all things is a totally separate issue from the debate as to whether He can lie, as the Deobandīs suggest. Such a comment is blasphemous to the utmost degree and a blatant ascription of a defect to Allāh. Debating whether an ordinary person can lie is a matter of disrespect, so how can someone see it respectful and fruitful to debate whether Allāh can lie?

Moreover, if this debate is allowed to flourish, it can lead to an avalanche of discussions which will subsequently undermine our position as Muslims. If Allāh can lie, does that mean He lied (God forbid) when He said there is a Paradise? Does this mean there is no Day of Judgement? [13]

1.4. Does Allāh have hands?

As mentioned earlier, one of the fundamental beliefs we hold about Allāh is that He does not resemble His creations; in essence, attributes or actions. However, there are several verses in the Qur'ān which seemingly suggest that He does share some similar attributes with His creation. For example, we are informed that;

- Allāh has a hand.

  'The hand of Allāh is above their hands.' (48: 10)

- Allāh can grasp with His hand.

  'And on the Day of Judgement the whole of the earth will be grasped by His hand and the heavens will be folded in His right hand...' (39:67)

---

12 p. 50. *al-Aqīda al-Hasana (al-Mar'ūf bi) Aqā'id al-Islām*. Hazrat Shāh Walī Allāh Muhaddith Delhvī.

13 p. 51. Ibid.

- Allāh has a face.

> 'Whoever is on it (the earth) will perish. And the face of your Lord full of majesty and honour will remain (forever).' (55: 26-27)

- Allāh can sit in some form on His Throne.

> 'Allāh is He who raised the skies without any pillars that you can see, then he became one with the Throne (*Istiwā*).' (13:2)

Such verses and others (where the interpretation becomes difficult) are called the *Mutashābis*. The reaction of the scholars and the pious ancestors to these verses has been mixed, but it can be summarised into three positions;

Position One.

- Some scholars believe that those who have *sufficient knowledge* on the matter are permitted to interpret such verses, and explain them in a matter befitting to Allāh's status. So for example, 'Allāh's hand' can be metaphorically interpreted as His power or care. The *Istiwā* on the Throne (*Arsh*) is interpreted as Allāh taking ownership of it.[14] This however is the minority position.

14 In the Qur'an (3:7) Allāh states that: 'He it is Who has revealed the Book to you; some of its verses are decisive, they are the basis of the Book, and others are allegorical; then as for those in whose hearts there is perversity they follow the part of it which is allegorical, seeking to mislead and seeking to give it (their own) interpretation. but none knows its interpretation except Allāh, and those who are firmly rooted in knowledge say: We believe in it, it is all from our Lord; and none do mind except those having understanding.' Those adhering to this position believe that the verse means Allāh *and* those 'firmly rooted' have knowledge in the allegorical verses. The majority opinion (as expressed in position two) is that there is a necessary pause after 'except Allāh' and that those 'firmly rooted' simply remark 'we believe in it' (*Ziā al-Qur'ān*, pp. 209-210. vol. I. Ziā al-Qur'ān Publications, Lahore, 1995)

Position Two; The correct and majority opinion.

- According to the majority of the Companions and the pious successors, such verses can only be truly interpreted by Allāh Almighty, and our task is simply to believe in the verses. So we say that the verses describing His hands and face are all truthful, but the exact form of it is beyond our comprehension.

Imām Mālik[15] (may Allāh be pleased with him) was asked about the verse which seemingly suggests that Allāh sat on the Throne. Imām Mālik replied:

الاستواء غير مجهول و الكيف غير معقول
و الايمان به واجب و السؤال عنه بدعة

> 'The sitting (*Istiwā*) is not known [by us]. Its exact form is not understandable. Faith in it is compulsory. And asking about it is *Bid'a*.'[16]

Imām Mālik then had the questioner thrown out of his gathering. This shows that it is not the way of the pious to indulge into what exactly these verses mean and entail. Our task is simply to believe in these verses.

Position Three; Sheikh Ibn Taymīyya and his followers.

- However, some Muslims have deviated from the overwhelming consensus by trying to ascribe human attributes to Allāh. Sheikh Ibn Taymīyya (d. 728/1328) gained notoriety amongst the scholars for

---

15 Imām Mālik ibn Anas (d. 179 A.H./795 C.E.). Major Hadīth scholar and jurist of Madina. He compiled the *al-Muwatta*, the Hadīth collection deemed as one of the most authentic compilations by Imām Shāfi'ī. The Māliki school of thought takes its names from him.

16 *Bid'a* means something that has been newly innovated in religion. Here, Imām Mālik used the term to mean that asking such a question contravenes the practice of the pious ancestors.

alleged anthropomorphism[17] and spent time in prison in Cairo because of such charges. He suggested that the Divine Names and Attributes of Allāh are to be taken at face value.[18] Because we raise our hands to the skies, he sought to suggest Allāh's presence there. He writes:

> 'Inclusive in what we have mentioned regarding the faith in Allāh is to believe in what He has informed us of regarding Himself in His book. And it is proven from the Messenger ﷺ and the Ummah have agreed on the fact that Allāh is above the skies on His Throne (*Arsh*), exalted over His creation.' [19]

Like our pious ancestors have purported, we raise our hands to the skies because this is the direction from which mercy and blessings descend, not because Allāh is present there (to the exclusion of other places).[20] When Ibrāhīm said 'I am going to my Lord' (37: 99), does this mean he knew His exact location? Of course not. Allāh created time and place, and thus He is free from them. He cannot be pinpointed and located to an exact place to the exclusion of others.

In short, there is no reason for Muslims to openly indulge in the exact form of Allāh's hand. Ibn Atā Allāh (d. 709/1309) offered priceless advice when he said:

> 'Allāh will not ask you about the details of His nature and His attributes; rather, He will ask you about what you did while you tarried on the earth. Therefore you should seek God where God seeks you.'[21]

---

17 Attributing human characteristics to Allāh.

18 p. 35. *Sharh al-Aqīdah al-Wāsita li Sheikh al-Islām Ibn Taymiyya*. Commentary by Muhammad ibn Sālih al-Athīmain.

19 p. 296. Ibid

20 p. 116. *al-Sharh al-Qawīm fī Hall Alfāz al-Sirāt al-Mustaqīm*. Abd Allāh al-Hararī.

21 p. 10. *The Creed of Imām al-Tahāwī. Translated, Introduced and Annotated by Hamza Yusuf.*

Imām Tahāwī (d. 321/933) warned:

> 'Whoever does not guard against denying [God's attributes] and against *Tashbīh* (anthropomorphism) has erred and failed to acquire understanding of divine transcendence (*Tanzīh*). For undoubtedly our Lord, the Sublime and Exalted, is described with the attributes of unity and uniqueness. No one in creation is in any way like Him.'[22]

Moreover, the Prophet ﷺ never asked and demanded Muslims to think about Allāh's existence and exact nature in great detail, and in fact pointed out that this could lead to misguidance and confusion. Imām Muslim (d. 261/874) reports in his *Sahīh*:

> Abū Huraira ؓ narrates that the Messenger of Allāh ﷺ said:
>
> 'The devil will come to one of you and ask: 'who created this and that?' until he will eventually ask: 'Then who created Allāh?' When it reaches this stage he should seek refuge with Allāh and refrain.'[23]

Allāh has only entrusted us with things we can fathom and comprehend. If something is behind our limited intellect and understanding (like for example, the *Rūh* (soul)), then it is not an essential element of our faith. Perhaps this is why the Prophet ﷺ ordered people to 'contemplate on Allāh's creation and do not contemplate on Allāh.'

To conclude, Allāh has ordered us to call Him by His 'beautiful names':

---

22 p. 58. Ibid.

23 *Sahīh Muslim*. Book of Faith. Hadīth no. 191. In a similar Hadīth, the Prophet (peace and blessings of Allāh be upon him) said:
'People will continue to ask one another until it is said: 'This [world], Allāh has created the universe, so who created Allāh?' So whosoever finds such [a thought] should say 'I believe in Allāh' (*Sahīh Muslim*. Book of Faith, Hadīth no. 190).

> 'And for Allāh are the most beautiful names, so call Him by them.' (7:180)

None of these names are controversial and difficult to understand. Certainly, none of them are anthropomorphic that result on confusion. In the same verse, Allāh orders us to:

> '...Leave the company of those who utter improper speech against His names. They will be requited for what they used to do.' (7:180)

Perhaps this is an implicit indication from our Lord to avoid discussions about Allāh's exact nature.

Moreover, one has to seriously question the academic worth of establishing the exact nature of Allāh's hand. When we learn about Allāh's mercy and His punishment, this will certainly increase our faith in Him. But if we establish the nature of Allāh's hand, will it increase our faith in Him? Will it make us fear Him more and be more obedient?

1.5. Is our intellect sufficient to acknowledge that Allāh exists?

This question refers to a famous, hypothetical debate that existed amongst the classical scholars. Allāh has sent a prophet or messenger to every single community that has existed to preach the message of Islām. But if there existed a community that never heard the message of Islām, would they still be expected to deduce the existence of Allāh through their own intellect?

- Many Shāfi'ī scholars believe that in the absence of messengers, it does not become incumbent upon people to accept faith. Imām al-Suyūtī (d.911/1505) wrote a separate essay on the faith of the Prophet's parents. In this work, he wrote that whosoever dies in the state that the message of Islām did not reach him, then he will be saved from the fire of Hell. This is because Allāh states in the Qur'ān:

> 'And We never punish until We have sent a messenger.' (17:15)[24]

- The majority of the Hanafī Sheikhs are of the opinion that if Allāh had not sent a messenger to us, we would still be expected to have faith in Allāh.[25] Imām Abū Hanīfa stated that our intellect should guide us to realise that this world must have a creator, and that this creator himself must not have been subject to creation.[26]

1.6. Conclusion.

Perhaps rightfully so, Allāh has not entrusted us with the responsibility to know His exact nature. He is an enigma that cannot be solved and an ocean whose depths cannot be reached. What we *do* need to know about Him is clearly and precisely defined in the Qur'ān and Sunna.

Sheikh Hamza Yūsuf once requested his Sheikh to be taught *Tawhīd*. He replied by simply reciting Sūrah Ikhlās and informing him that this

---

24 p. 32. *Sharh al-Risāla al-Nāfi'a wa al-Hujaj al-Qāti'a*. Sheikh Muhammad Abd al-Latīf Sālih al-Farfūr (d. 1407/1986).

25 p. 31. Ibid.

26 In the past, people could and did deduce the oneness of God through their own intellect, like Plato and his disciple Aristotle. Aristotle had some interesting views concerning theology, the one most worthy of attention is the state of nature, or *physis*, in his book *The Politics*. According to Aristotle, the nature of something is its 'end' or what it is when it is fully developed. What each thing is when its growth is completed we call the nature of the thing, whether it be a man, a horse or the family. An acorn is at its most perfect point of the cycle of life when it blossoms into an oak tree. A caterpillar is to be considered as at its peak when it becomes a beautiful butterfly. Every living thing in this universe is part of this nature. At all times things are coming into being and passing away, the movement is from potentiality to fulfilment and then decay. Hence, according to Aristotle, everything is subject to a motion, or cycle. But most importantly there would be no motion at all unless there is first a force of movement that is itself unmoved- namely God. Essentially there must have been a being which initiated and started this cycle in all living things, and that being itself is not subject to motion or a cycle. That being is God.

was sufficient as a lesson on *Tawhīd*. It is important to note how we are instructed to know this Sūrah through the means of the Prophet ﷺ (i.e. *Qul, 'say'*) and not through our own intellect.

On a final note, the Wahhābī movement claim that they are the champions of *Tawhīd*. But as we have seen, they have made fundamental errors and indeed blasphemous remarks in this discipline.

Chapter Two

Understanding *Shirk*

2.0. *Shirk*- Introduction.

Shirk (شرك) literally means 'to associate' or 'to partner'. In Islām, it is to associate somebody or something in Allāh's inherent nature or in any of His attributes. This is the greatest of all crimes according to Allāh, as the Qur'ān states that He is willing to forgive all types of sins except *Shirk* (4:116). This fact is sufficient to warn us of the magnitude of this crime. Murder, rape, theft, burglary, deceit – all can eventually be forgiven by Allāh, but not *Shirk*.

2.1. Defining *Shirk*; Imām al-Qurtubī's definition.

The Qur'ānic scholar Allāma Qurtubī (d. 671 A.H./1272 C.E.) offers a detailed definition of *Shirk* in his Tafsīr, *al-Jāmi' li Ahkām al-Qur'ān*.[27] He writes that there are three different stages or forms of *Shirk*, and all three are forbidden (*Harām*). (i) To consider a being other than Allāh (a tree, idol, person, jinn etc.) worthy of worship. This is the major form of *Shirk*, and the

27 Pīr Muhammad Karam Shāh al-Azharī (may Allāh shower His mercy upon him) has cited this in *Ziā al-Qur'ān*, (vol. I: pp. 351-2).

type of *Shirk* committed by the people of the Jāhiliyya period.[28] (ii) To consider that another being other than Allāh can perform and create certain actions independently (without Allāh), even if the person does not believe that that person or being is a God. For example, Nimrūd, who was the enemy of Ibrāhīm (peace be upon him), believed that he could 'give life and cause death' (2:258). (iii) Lastly, *Shirk* in worship, and this is *Riyā* (showing off). This too is a form of *Shirk* because the worship is not being done for the sake of Allāh anymore. It is sometimes referred to as *Shirk Khafī* (hidden polytheism). Though this form is still forbidden, it is the least severe of the three because the one who indulges in it is not declared a non-Muslim.

From this we can appreciate that *Shirk* is when someone (i) ascribes a partner to Allāh in His essence or attributes (ii) with the knowledge and belief that this being or object is worthy of such accolade and that it can be done independently of Allāh.

2.2. Defining *Shirk*; the Wahhābī interpretation.

Muhammad ibn Abd al-Wahhāb (d. 1207/1792)[29] writes in *al-Usūl al-Thalātha*:

> 'The greatest thing that Allāh has ordered is *Tawhīd*; this is to single out Allāh alone for worship. And the greatest thing He has forbidden is *Shirk*; and this is calling other than Him with Him (و هو دعوة غيره معه).'[30]

28 The period prior to the Prophet's announcement of prophecy is known as *Jāhiliyya*, which means 'ignorance'.

29 Muhammad ibn Abd al-Wahhāb (1703-1792) was a Muslim scholar who preached an extremist version of Islām in the Arab Peninsula during the eighteenth century. Today his legacy is popularly known as Wahhābism.

30 pp. 25-6. *Al-Usūl al-Thalātha*. Muhammad ibn Abd al-Wahhāb.

Muhammad Nāsir al-Dīn Albānī (d. 1419/1999) writes:

> 'There are three types of *Shirk*. The first is *Shirk* in Godliness (*Rabūbiyya*). This is to believe that there is another creator with Allāh Almighty...and this type of *Shirk* in this Ummah is less, *al-Hamdu Lillāh*. The second type of *Shirk* is *Shirk* in deity-ness (*al-Alūhiyya*) and worship (*al-Abūdiyya*). And this is that someone other than Allāh is worshipped, namely the Prophets and pious ones (*Sālihīn*), in the form of seeking assistance from them (*Istighātha*) and proclaiming them in times of difficulty and its likes. With great regret, this is common in this Ummah... And the third is *Shirk* in attributes (*al-Sifat*). This is when some of the creations of Allāh are ascribed with attributes exclusive to Allāh alone, like the knowledge of the unseen (*Ghaib*). This type [of *Shirk*] is common amongst many of the Sufīs, like the saying of some of them [namely Imām Busīrī];
>
> > *And from parts of your generosity [O Muhammad] are the world and the hereafter.*
> >
> > *And from your knowledge is the knowledge of the Tablet and Pen.*' [31]

Ibn Sa'dī (d. 1376/1957) wrote in the commentary of Muhammad ibn Abd al-Wahhāb's *Kitāb al-Tawhīd,* under the chapter 'he who seeks *Tabarruk*[32] with a tree or stone or its like':

> 'This is from [the forms of] *Shirk* and it is the actions of the polytheists. For verily the scholars have agreed that it is not part of Sharī'ah to seek *Tabarruk* with anything from the trees,

31 pp. 7-8. Muhammad Nāsir al-Dīn Albānī (d. 1419/1999) in *al-Aqīdah al-Tahāwiyya, Sharh wa Ta'līq*.

32 *Tabarruk* means to seek blessings.

> stones, places, Islamic sites and its likes...this is the major *Shirk*. This (principle) is universal in everything from the Station of Ibrahim (*Maqām Ibrāhīm*), the room of the Prophet ﷺ, to the stone of Bayt al-Maqdas [in Jerusalem] and other excellent places.' [33]

In the same book, Ibn Abd al-Wahhāb includes a chapter titled 'what has been mentioned in slaughtering for other than Allāh':

> 'This is *Shirk*...slaughtering in the name of a being other than Allāh is the major *Shirk* and excludes one from the circle of Islām.'[34]

Further on he writes:

> '...and major *Shirk* is like praying to the people of the graves, and seeking help through them (*Istighātha*) and praying for worldly and heavenly matters...this is exactly what the idol-worshippers do with their idols.' [35]

To summarise, according to the followers of Muhammad ibn Abd al-Wahhāb, the following are all considered *Shirk*:

- Calling anyone other than Allāh (like proclaiming *Yā Rasūllāh*) for *Istighātha* (seeking help).
- Seeking the Prophet's *Wasīla* (medium).
- to suggest that the Prophet (peace and blessings of Allāh be upon him) has *Ilm Ghaib* (knowledge of the unseen).

---

33 p. 39. *Kitāb al-Tawhīd wa Kitāb al-Qawl al-Sadīd*. Muhammad ibn Abd al-Wahhāb, commentary by Abd al-Rahmān ibn Nāsir ibn Sa'dī.

34 p. 41. Ibid.

35 pp. 65-6. Ibid.

- to seek blessings (*Tabarruk*) from Islamic relics.
- to slaughter in the name of someone other than Allāh.
- visiting the shrines of Allāh's pious servants. Muhammad ibn Abd al-Wahhāb was vehemently against people visiting Madina Sharif in order to greet the Prophet ﷺ.

2.3. Understanding *Shirk*.

To truly understand what *Shirk* is, it is important to highlight Islām's concept of worship, or *Ibāda*. All scholars agree that *Ibāda* is 'utmost humility and humbleness'. A simple example would be that of prostration in Salāh. Sajda certainly shows humility and humbleness but this is not the only part of Salāh which is considered as worship; to stand up with the hands tied, to perform Rukū, to return from the Rukū position with the hands on the side, to sit and to turn the face right and left after Salām are all part of Salāh and thus all considered as worship. If all the acts of Salāh are considered as worship, then when a student sits with his hands on his laps in the presence of his Sheikh, or when a child stands for his father, then is it possible to say that the student and the child are worshipping the Sheikh and father respectively? Of course not. We must remember that Jibrā'īl sat in exactly the same way in front of the Prophet ﷺ when he famously asked him questions about Islām, Īmān and Ihsān.[36]

Therefore the question is what has made these acts – when performed in Salāh – a form of worship, and the very same acts – when performed in the presence of a Sheikh or father – something other than worship? The answer is simple; it all depends on what the person really thinks and believes in his mind when he performs these acts in front of the

---

36 *Sahīh Muslim*, Book of Faith, Hadīth no.9.

being. If he sits in the Qa'da (sitting) position with the firm belief that he is worshipping Allāh, then it is considered as *Ibāda* and he is showing 'utmost humility and humbleness' whilst doing so. But if he sits in the Qa'da position in front of his Sheikh and firmly believes that he is a servant of Allāh, and that he is not intending to worship him, then this will be interpreted as respect, dignity and honour for the Sheikh, but not worship.[37]

It is therefore clear from this that no-one or nothing is worthy of worship other than Allāh Almighty. He is the most Able and all-Knowing. He is the Creator and Sustainer of all. He alone possesses the power to forgive and punish. And only when someone truly *believes* that a being other than Allāh is worthy of worship and able to perform actions reserved for him alone does he become a *Mushrik* (polytheist).

2.4. Refuting the Wahhābī position.

Certainly, if someone truly believes that the Prophet ﷺ can answer our Duās to the exclusion of Allāh, and that he possesses the knowledge of the unseen independently and without the assistance of Allāh, then this is *Shirk*. If a person believes that something can be done independently without the will of Allāh, then this is polytheism. But this is not what the Ahl al-Sunna claims and believes. Also, we do not believe – like Muhammad Nāsir al-Dīn Albānī thinks we do – that 'the Prophets and pious ones (*Sālihīn*)' are worthy of worship. What follows is a brief refutation of the Wahhābis' interpretation of *Shirk*.

37 Having said this, the Prophet (peace and blessings of Allāh be upon him) did clearly forbid prostrating to anyone other than Allāh. So this is prohibited in all of its forms, regardless of intention.

2.4.1. Calling anyone other than Allāh' (like proclaiming *Yā Rasūllāh*) for *Istighātha* (seeking help)

- If saying *Yā Rasūllāh* is *Shirk,* then the Companions committed *Shirk* when they would proclaim 'Yā Muhammad' before going into battle. This was after the Prophet ﷺ physically left this world.[38]

- If saying *Yā Rasūllāh* is *Shirk,* then the Companion Bilāl ibn Hārith Muzannī committed *Shirk* when he came to the grave of the Prophet ﷺ and said: 'O Messenger of Allāh! Please pray for rain for the sake of your Ummah, because they are being destroyed as a result of the drought.' This was in the caliphate of Umar ﷺ.[39]

- If *Istighātha* from beings other than Allāh was forbidden, then we

---

38 The Muslims were engaged in a fierce battle with Musailma Kazzāb during the Battle of Yamāma. Allāma Ibn Athīr describes the events as follows:
'Then Khālid ibn Walīd challenged the enemies to fight. Thus according to the [established] practice of the Muslims, they proclaimed *Yā Muhammadau* loudly. They then killed all those who challenged them to fight' (*Al-Kāmil fi al-Tārikh*). Hāfiz Ibn Kathīr also recorded the same report (*Al-Bidāya wa al-Nihāya*). Both Ibn Athīr and Ibn Kathīr have clarified that it was the established practice of the Companions and Successors to proclaim *Yā Muhammadau* loudly in times of difficulty and hardship. The Muslims who deny the legitimacy of such calls are the same ones who respect the opinion of Ibn Kathīr immensely. Hence, this quote is strong evidence against their view. (pp. 155-156. *A Commentary of Sūrah Fātiha based on Tibyān al-Qur'ān*. Allāma Ghulām Rasūl Sa'īdī. Translated by Ather Hussain al-Azhari).

39 There was a severe drought in a particular year during the caliphate of Umar (may Allāh be pleased with him). Bilāl ibn Hārith Muzannī (may Allāh be pleased with him) came to the resting place of the Messenger and requested him to pray for rain on behalf of his Ummah. Hāfiz Ibn Abū Shaiba reports with his chain:
'Mālik al-Dār, who was the food minister for Umar (may Allāh be pleased with him), reports that during Umar's caliphate, a drought inflicted the people. One person (Bilāl ibn Hārith Muzannī) went to the resting place of the Prophet (peace and blessings of Allāh be upon him) and said: 'O Messenger of Allāh! Please pray for rain for the sake of your Ummah, because they are being destroyed as a result of the drought.'
The Prophet appeared in the dream of this person and said: 'Go to Umar; offer my salutations to him and tell him that undoubtedly rain will descend upon you. And tell him: 'Be clever! Be clever!
The man went to Umar and told him what happened. Umar began to cry and remarked: 'O Allāh! I spare no effort except in what escapes my power' (*Al-Musannaf*). Ibn Kathīr has reported the above incident almost identically in his work *al-Bidāya wa al-Nihāya* (pp. 134-5. *A Commentary of Sūrah Fātiha based on Tibyān al-Qur'ān*. Allāma Ghulām Rasūl Sa'īdī. Translated by Ather Hussain al-Azhari).

would not have been taught to say *Yā Ibād Allāh A'īnūnī* (O servants of Allāh! Help me!) when we come across difficulties in our travels.[40]

2.4.2. Seeking the Prophet's *Wasīla* (medium).

- If seeking the *Wasīla* of the Prophet ﷺ was forbidden, then:

(i) Ādam (peace be upon him) would not have sought forgiveness through the Prophet's *Wasīla*.[41]

(ii) the Prophet ﷺ would not have taught his own Companions Du'ās in which his *Wasīla* is taken.[42]

---

40 Hāfiz Abū Bakr Dinūrī, known more famously by the title Ibn al-Sinni, reports: 'Ibn Mas'ūd (may Allāh be pleased with him) narrates that the Prophet (peace and blessings of Allāh be upon him) said: 'When the transporting [animal] of one of you disappears in a foreign land, then you should say: 'O the pious servants of Allāh! Stop [the animal]! O the pious servants of Allāh! Stop [the animal]!' This is because on earth there are Allāh's servants who can stop it.' (*Aml Yaum wa Laila*; cited in *A Commentary of Sūrah Fātiha based on Tibyān al-Qur'ān*. Allāma Ghulām Rasūl Sa'īdī. Translated by Ather Hussain al-Azhari, p. 152).

41 Imām Baihaqī reports with his chain:
'Umar (may Allāh be pleased with him) narrates that the Prophet (peace and blessings of Allāh be upon him) said: 'When Ādam committed the mistake, he said to Allāh: 'O Allāh! In the name of Muhammad I ask you to forgive me.' Allāh asked: 'O Ādam! How do you know of Muhammad when I have not yet [physically] created him yet?' Ādam replied: 'O Allāh! When You were creating me and blew the spirit into me, I looked up to the *Arsh* (throne) and I saw inscribed *Lā Ilāha Illallāhu Muhammadur Rasūl Allāh*. I knew then that the person whose name is coupled with Yours is the most beloved of creations.' Allāh replied: 'Ādam, you have said the truth. He is the most beloved of My creations and I have forgiven you because you have asked Me with his *Wasīla*. Had I not created Muhammad, I would not have created you at all.' (*Dalā'il al-Nabūwwa*; cited in *A Commentary of Sūrah Fātiha based on Tibyān al-Qur'ān*. Allāma Ghulām Rasūl Sa'īdī. Translated by Ather Hussain al-Azhari, p. 127.

42 Uthmān ibn Hunaif (may Allāh be pleased with him) reports that a blind man came to the Prophet (peace and blessings of Allāh be upon him) and said: 'O Prophet of Allāh! Please pray to Allāh to return my sight.' The Prophet said: 'If you wish, I shall pray to Allāh, but if you wish you can endure it, for that is better for you.' The blind man replied: 'O Allāh's Messenger! My blindness causes me great hardship.' The Prophet told him: 'Go and perform ablution. Then perform two Rak'ats of Salāh and then pray, 'O Allāh! I ask You and I turn to You by the *Wasīla* of our Prophet Muhammad! I turn to my Lord by your *Wasīla* for my need, so that it might be fulfilled. O Allāh! Grant the Prophet intercession for me.' This Hadīth has also been recorded by Imām Tirmidhī, Imām Ahmad, Imām Hākim and Ibn Asākir. (pp. 131-132. *A Commentary of Sūrah Fātiha based on Tibyān al-Qur'ān*. Allāma Ghulām Rasūl Sa'īdī. Translated by Ather Hussain al-Azhari).

(iii) the Companions would not have performed Du'ās using his *Wasīla* after he left this world.[43]

2.4.3. To suggest that the Prophet ﷺ has *Ilm Ghaib* (knowledge of the unseen).

No one from the Sunni Muslims hold the belief that the Prophet ﷺ has knowledge of the unseen independently. Pīr Karam Shāh al-Azharī (d. 1418/1998) explains our position:

> 'Our belief is that Allāh Almighty inundated the Prophet's ﷺ heart with knowledge of the unseen. However, the Prophet's knowledge – in comparison to Allāh's – is not his own, nor is

43 Uthmān ibn Hunaif reports that a man repeatedly visited Uthmān [Ibn Affān] concerning something he needed, but Uthmān did not pay attention to him or his need. Thus the man complained to Uthmān [ibn Hunaif], who said to him: 'Perform ablution and visit the Holy Prophet's Mosque, and perform two Rak'ats of Salāh therein and then read this *Du'ā*,
'O Allāh! I ask You and I turn to You by the *Wasīla* of our Prophet Muhammad! I turn to my Lord by your *Wasīla* for my need, so that it might be fulfilled. O Allāh! Grant the Prophet intercession for me.'
The man did as he was instructed and then went to Uthmān's [Ibn Affān] door. The doorman came, grabbed him by the hand and took him to Uthmān, who treated him with great respect and seated him on his cushion. Uthmān asked him: 'What do you need?' and the man mentioned what he wanted, and Uthmān fulfilled it for him. Then he said to him: 'I hadn't remembered your need until now; whenever you need something just mention it.'
The man then departed and met Uthmān ibn Hunaif and thanked him saying: 'May Allāh reward you, for you spoke to Uthmān ibn Affān [on my behalf].' Uthmān ibn Hunaif replied: 'By Allāh! I did not speak to him. But I was once present in the Holy Prophet's company and I saw a blind man come to him, complaining of his sight-loss. The Prophet said: 'If you wish, I shall pray to Allāh, but if you wish you can endure it, for that is better for you.' The man replied: 'O Allāh's Messenger! I do not have anyone to lead me around and it causes me great hardship.' The Prophet then instructed him 'perform ablution, then perform two Rak'ats Salāh and pray the following [*Du'ā*].' Uthmān ibn Hunaif said: 'It was not long after the blind man returned to us as if nothing had ever been wrong with his eyes!'
Hafiz Zakī al-Dīn Abd al-Azīm ibn Abd al-Qawī Munzirī (d. 656 A.H.) has recorded this Hadīth in *al-Targhīb wa al-Tarhīb*. It has also been mentioned by Hāfiz al-Haithamī in *Majma al-Zawā'id*, who declares the report as *Sahīh* (authentic). (pp. 136-137. *A Commentary of Sūrah Fātiha based on Tibyān al-Qur'ān*. Allāma Ghulām Rasūl Sa'īdī. Translated by Ather Hussain al-Azhari).

it infinite. Rather, it is merely given from Allāh. In comparison to Allāh's knowledge, the Prophet's knowledge is not even a particle of sand to the whole desert, or a drop in the ocean. In comparison to the knowledge of the rest of humanity, the Prophet's knowledge is a huge ocean whose depth has not been explored, and whose shores have not been reached.'[44]

2.4.4. To seek blessings *(Tabarruk)* from Islamic relics

- The son of Imām Ahmad ibn Hanbal reports that:

سألت أبي عن الرجل يمس منبر رسول الله صلي الله عليه و سلم و يتبرك بمسه و يقبله و يفعل بالقبر مثل ذالك رجاء ثواب الله تعالي قال لا باس به

'I asked my father Ahmad ibn Hanbal about a person who wipes the pulpit of the Messenger of Allāh ﷺ, seeks blessings (*Baraka*) by wiping it, kisses it and does the same with the grave, all with the hope of a reward from Allāh. Ahmad ibn Hanbal replied: 'There is no harm in this.'[45]

Ahmad ibn Hanbal (d. 241/855) did not object to this practice because there was no intention of worshipping someone or something other than Allāh.

- Umm Salma (may Allāh be pleased with her) possessed some blessed hairs of the Prophet ﷺ. When people were ill or affected by the evil eye, then they would come to her with water in a basin. She would then

44 Vol. I, p. 301, *Ziā al-Qur'ān*, Pīr Muhammad Karam Shāh (1918-1998).
45 p. 112. *Tashīh al-Aqā'id*. Muhammad Abd al-Hāmid Budāyūnī.

dip the hairs of the Prophet in the water. They would then drink this water or bathe from it as a means of *Shifā*.[46]

- Anas ibn Mālik requested to be buried with the hairs of the Prophet ﷺ under his tongue. [47]

- Mu'āwiya possessed the shirt, nails and hairs of the Prophet ﷺ. He asked to be buried with these relics. When he made this bequest he remarked: 'If anything will benefit me [in the grave], then these relics will.' [48]

Umm Salma, Anas and Mu'āwiya (may Allāh be pleased with him) knew that it was Allāh Almighty who put the blessings in these items. This is why respecting the religious relics is not *Shirk*. If the Companions found cure in drinking from the water dipped in the Prophet's blessed hair, it was because Allāh put the cure in it.

2.4.5. To slaughter in the name of someone other than Allāh.

Abū Talha related that the Prophet ﷺ sacrificed one ram, and while sacrificing the other he said: 'This is on behalf of every one of my Ummah who believe in me and testified (to my prophethood).' [49]

The sacrifice is done for the sake of Allāh and for the sake of His worship. As the above Hadīth shows, there is no harm in *dedicating* the reward to one of His creations.

---

46 *Sahīh al-Bukhārī.* Book of Clothes. Hadīth no. 5446.
47 p. 16. *Tabarruk al-Sahāba bi Āthār Rasūl Allāh.* Sheikh Muhammad Tāhir ibn Abd al-Qādir ibn Mahmūd al-Kurdī.
48 p. 24. Ibid
49 Recorded by Imām Tabarānī.

2.4.6. Imām Busīrī; a *Mushrik*?

Unreservedly, Muhammad Nāsir al-Dīn Albānī decreed Imām Busīrī a *Mushrik* for the contents of his *Burdah*.[50] This does not explain why the Prophet ﷺ appeared in his dream and cured him from his paralysis. One cannot imagine for a moment that our Messenger would appear in the dream of an apostate.

Ibn Taymiyya (d.728/1327) said:

> 'Muhammad is the chief of the children of Ādam, the best of creation, the noblest of them in the sight of Allāh. This is why some have said 'were it not for him, Allāh would not have created a throne, nor a Footstool, nor a heaven, earth, sun or moon.'[51]

In short, some Muslims blindly interpret permitted acts as *Shirk*, though literally and Islamically, such claims are baseless. The Prophet ﷺ himself never envisaged that his followers would be subject to the wrath of *Shirk*, so it is strange that the Wahhābī movement thinks otherwise.

Imām Bukhārī (d. 256/869) reports from Uqba ibn Āmir ﷺ who said:

> 'Indeed the Prophet ﷺ left one day and performed Salāh on the People of Uhud, the Salāh of the deceased. Then he turned to the pulpit and said:
>
> 'I am preceding you; and I am a witness over you. And indeed, by Allāh, I am undoubtedly looking towards the *Hawdh* [right] now. And indeed I have been given the keys to the treasures of

---

50 The *Burdah* is the famous poem written by Imām Busīrī (d. 694/1294) in praise of the Prophet.

51 Cited by Jibrīl Haddād in *Hadīth of Ādam's Tawwasul through the Prophet*, April 2006 (www.livingislam.org).

the earth, or the keys of the earth. And verily, I do not fear that you will commit polytheism after me. But I verily fear you will dispute with one another in it (i.e. the world).'[52]

In short, if the Prophet ﷺ did not fear his Ummah would commit polytheism after him, why do these Muslims think it is a problem of epidemic proportions? Do these people purport that – God forbid – the Prophet's prediction and analysis was wrong and that they are right? Do they think that they know and understand the religion of Allāh better than the Beloved Prophet, who, in the words of this Hadīth, had been given the keys to the treasures of the earth?

2.5. *Takfīr*: the issue of declaring others infidels.

To propagate his beliefs, Muhammad ibn Abd al-Wahhāb directed all the verses in the Qur'ān referring to the polytheists of Makka to the mainstream Muslims, something which continues today. No other Qur'ānic commentator prior to him suggested that these verses were revealed regarding the Muslims. It is wrong and wholly incorrect to direct the verses revealed regarding the pagan Arabs towards the Muslims. The polytheists of the Prophet's time:

- actually considered their idols worthy of worship.
- actually believed that the idols could help them to the exclusion of Allāh.

As a result of this view on *Tawhīd* and *Shirk*, Muhammad ibn Abd al-Wahhāb viewed any Muslim who did not agree with his sect as a *Mushrik*

52 *Sahīh al-Bukharī* (Chapter; the prayer upon the martyr; Hadīth no. 1258: Chapter; *Uhud* loves us and we love *Uhud*. Hadīth no. 3776: Chapter; the *Hawdh* (Pool), Hadīth no. 6102; Chapter; what is warned against from the fruits of the world and dispute within it. Hadīth no. 5946), *Sahīh Muslim* (Book of Superiorities; Chapter; the proving of the *Hawdh* of our Prophet; Hadīth no. 4248), *Musnad Ahmad* (The chains of the Shāmīs, The reports of Uqba ibn Āmir, Hadīth no. 16705).

(polytheist) or *Kāfir* (non-believer). Stephen Schwarz writes:

> 'The essence of Ibn Abd al-Wahhāb's preaching came down to three points. First, ritual is superior to intention. Second, no reverence for the dead is permitted. Third, there can be no intercessory prayer, addressed to God by means of the Prophet or saints...Prayers to God by means of a pious person or even honours to any individual other than God were condemned as idolatry, despite their acceptance by all previous generations of Muslims and the Prophet himself...
>
> ...He demanded that the Muslim profession of faith (i.e. the *Kalima*) be made a second time, as an adherent of his Wahhābī sect.' [53]

Later, Schwarz writes:

> 'Ibn Abd al-Wahhāb is said to have killed a blind Muezzin who insisted on praying for the Prophet at the conclusion of his summons to worship (i.e. *Azān*), as required by the four established legal schools....He denounced his opponents, and all Muslims unwilling to accept his views, as idolaters and apostates, and abused the prophets, scholars, saints and other pious figures of the past. Al-Zahawi states that Ibn Abd al-Wahhāb 'made no secret' of his opinion that all Muslims had fallen unto unbelief and that if they did not follow him, they should all be killed, their wives and daughters violated and their possessions confiscated.' [54]

Muhammad ibn Abd al-Wahhāb's own brother Sulaimān ibn Abd al-Wahhāb was one of the biggest critics of this new school of thought. He

---

53 p. 69. *The Two Faces of Islām: The House of Sa'ud from Tradition to Terror*. Stephen Schwarz.
54 pp. 70-71. Ibid.

wrote a book called *al-Sawā'iq al-Ilāhiyya fī al-Radd alā al-Wahhābiyya*, in which he highlighted the misguided nature of his brother's version of Islām. In his Friday *Khutba* (sermon), Muhammad ibn Abd al-Wahhāb would every week declare that 'whosoever seeks the Wasīla of the Prophet has become a Kāfir.' His brother Sulaimān approached him regarding this and asked him: 'How many pillars of Islām are there O Muhammad ibn Abd al-Wahhāb?' He replied: 'Five.' Sulaimān said: 'You have made a sixth pillar; that whoever does not follow you, is not a Muslim. This, according to you, is the sixth pillar of Islām.'[55]

To call a Muslim a non-Muslim is a serious crime which can result in damning repercussions for the one who utters such a remark. The Prophet ﷺ warned in a Hadīth reported by Ibn Umar ﵁:

> 'Whoever says to his brother 'O infidel!', then the statement returns to one of them.' [56]

55 p. 137. *al-Durar al-Sanniya fī al-Radd ala al-Wahhabiyya*. Sayyid Ahmad ibn al-Sayyid Zaini Dahlan.

56 *Sahīh al-Bukhārī*. Book of Adab (manners), Hadīth no. 5639. In other words, when one makes a statement as such and cannot prove why he is a non-Muslim conclusively, then the speaker himself becomes a non-believer.

Chapter Three

Belief in Angels

3.0. Angels - Introduction.

As Muslims, we are required to believe that Allāh has created angels (*Malak*, plural: *Malā'ika*), all with different forms and different tasks. In the Holy Qur'ān, Allāh states:

> 'The Messenger believes in what has been sent down to him from his Lord, and so do the believers. Each one believes in Allāh, His angels, and His messengers...' (2:285)

If a person refuses to believe in the existence of angels, then he is no longer considered a Muslim.

3.1. The key attributes of angels.

From the Qur'ān and Sunna, we are able to identify some of the key features of angels:

i. Allāh created the angels from *Nūr* (light).[57]

---

57 *Sahīh Muslim*. Book of Zuhd & Raqā'iq, Hadīth no. 5314.

ii. They have been created to be obedient. In order words, they cannot perform any act contrary to the will of Allāh. The Qur'ān states that: 'The angels fear their Lord above them and they do what they are commanded' (16: 50). Metaphorically, we sometimes say 'x is like an angel', to denote his/her innocence.

iii. They do not eat or drink.

iv. They are not male or female. This refutes the claim of the pagan Arabs who would characterise the angels as being female.

v. They are hidden from the sights of ordinary Muslims.

vi. They can change into different forms, as Allāh wishes. For example, Jibrā'īl once appeared as a man in white clothes in the presence of the Prophet.[58]

vii. Only Allāh knows their exact number (74: 31). In order, to give us an idea of their vast number, we have been informed that 70,000 angels perform *Tawāf* around the *Bayt Ma'mūr* (the Ka'ba in the heavens) each and every day, never to return again.[59]

3.2. The duties of the four, prominent angels.

Allāh Almighty has allocated angels to perform certain duties. The most prominent angels are four: Jibrā'īl, Mīkā'īl, Isrā'īl, and Isrāfīl (peace be upon them).

---

58 *Sahīh Muslim*, Book of Faith, Hadīth no. 9.
59 *Sahīh al-Bukhārī*. Book of the beginning of the creation, Hadīth no. 2968.

i. Jibrā'īl (peace be upon him).

He is the angel of revelation for the Prophets; his duty is to deliver the word of Allāh to the prophets and messengers.

Jibrā'īl can take on many forms, but only the Prophet ﷺ saw him in his original, created form. Regarding the verse 'And surely he saw the messenger on the bright horizon' (81:19-23), Ibn Hajar (d. 852/1448) writes that it refers to when the Prophet ﷺ saw Jibrā'īl with six-hundred wings on the bright horizon.

ii. Mīkā'īl (peace be upon him).

He is the angel of rain; he controls the clouds and moves them to wherever Allāh wants them. He is also in charge of *Rizq* (sustenance).

iii. Isrā'īl (peace be upon him).

He is the angel who takes the souls at the time of death. The Qur'ān states:

> 'Say (O Messenger!): 'The angel of death, who is set over you, will [one day] take your souls, then you shall be brought to your Lord.' (32: 11)

iv. Isrāfīl (peace be upon him).

He is the angel who will blow the horn on the Day of Judgement. In a Hadīth recorded by Imām Tirmidhī, the Prophet ﷺ informed us that ever since he was entrusted with this responsibility from Allāh, he has had the horn in his lips with his cheeks blown, ready to blow it.[60]

---

60 *Sunan al-Tirmidhī*. Book of Tafsīr of the Qur'ān, Chapter: Sūrah Zumar, Hadīth no. 3166.

3.3. The duties of other angels.

Other angels and their duties include:

i. The two writers; *Raqīb* and *Atīd* (also called *Kirāman Kātibīn*). The Qur'ān states:

> 'And indeed over you (are appointed angels) to watch you. *Kirāman Kātibīn*. They know all that you do.' (82: 10-12)

Raqīb writes all the good deeds on the right side and *Atīd* writes all the bad things on the left. Of the two, the angel of good deeds (*Raqīb*) has more authority. So if the Muslim intends a wrongful act, *Raqīb* orders the writer of bad things not to write it immediately. He orders him to allow the Muslim time so that he may remember Allāh or seek forgiveness. If he does seek forgiveness or remember Allāh then he saves himself from sin.

ii. *Munkar* and *Nakīr*, who are the two angels that ask the three questions in the grave.

iii. Some angels are entrusted with enforcing Allāh's wrath and anger over sinful people.

iv. There are angels who formulate the physical features of the baby in the womb of the mother and infuse life into it.

v. Some are entrusted to protect Allāh's pious servants.

vi. Some are entrusted with guarding Paradise and welcoming its inhabitants. Allāh states in the Qur'ān:

> 'And those who were conscious of their Lord will proceed towards Paradise in great numbers, and when they reach it, they shall find its gates wide open and its keepers (the angels) will say to them: 'Peace be upon you! You have done well; enter this Paradise forever.' (39: 73)

vii. Some angels appear on earth during special, religious events. For example, Abū Huraira ﷺ reports that the Prophet ﷺ said:

> 'On every Friday, the angels take their stand at every gate of the mosque to write the names of the people according to the time of their arrival for Friday prayer. And when the Imām sits (on the pulpit for the sermon), they fold up their scrolls and get ready to listen to the sermon.'[61]

viii. The *Sayyāhūn*.

In a Hadīth recorded by Imām al-Nasā'ī (d. 303/915) in his *Sunan*, the Prophet ﷺ said:

> 'For Allāh are travelling (*Sayyāhūn*) angels on earth, [whose task] is to pass on the Salām of my Ummah to me.'[62]

Similarly, there are angels who roam the earth looking for people who collectively engage in the *Zikr* of Allāh.[63]

ix. There are appointed angels whose task is to protect Madina Sharif.

---

61 *Sahīh Muslim*. Book of Jum'a. Hadīth no. 1417.

62 *Sunan al-Nasā'ī*. Book of Sahv (forgetfulness), Chapter, Salām upon the Prophet. Hadīth no. 1265. The same Hadīth has also been recorded by Imām Ahmad (Hadīth no. 3484) in his *Musnad* and Imām Dārmī in his *Sunan* (Hadīth no. 2655).

63 *Sahīh al-Bukhārī*, Book of supplications, Chapter: the superiority of Allāh's remembrance. Also cited on pp. 29-30 in *Al-Muntakhabāt al-Imdādiyya*. M.I.H. Pirzada.

The Prophet ﷺ explained:

لا يدخل المدينة رعب المسيح الدجال و لها
يومئذ سبعة أبواب علي كل باب ملكان

> 'Dajjāl will not enter into Madina. On that day [when he attempts to] there will be seven entrances [to the city], each one guarded by two angels.'[64]

x. Some angels participate in congregational prayer and say Āmīn as the Muslims do. In a Hadīth recorded by Imām Nasā'ī in his *Sunan*, the Prophet ﷺ said:

> 'When one from amongst you reads Āmīn, then the angels of the sky (too) read Āmīn. Thus when the Āmīn of the Muslims coincides with the Āmīn of the angels, the sins of the Muslims are forgiven.'[65]

xi. The angels have different duties, different ranks and different forms; but *all* have the duty to perform Salām upon the Prophet ﷺ. Allāh states:

> 'Verily Allāh and His angels send blessings upon the Prophet. O Believers! Send blessings and Salām upon him abundantly.' (33:56) [66]

---

64 *Sahīh al-Bukhārī*. Book of *Fitan*, Chapter: the mentioning of Dajjāl, Hadīth no. 6592.

65 *Sunan al-Nasā'ī*. Book of the opening (of Prayer), Chapter: the Imam's loud recitation of Amīn, Hadīth no. 916. Cited on p. 185. in *A Commentary of Sūrah Fātiha based on Tibyān al-Qur'ān*. Allāma Ghulām Rasūl Sa'īdī. Translated by Ather Hussain al-Azhari.

66 Closer examination of this verse reveals that the word *Malā'ika* (angels) is a plural, its singular being *Malak*. It is followed by a *Hū* pronoun which indicates and refers back to Allāh Almighty (i.e. *His Angels*). As a rule of Arabic grammar when a plural is possessed by a personal pronoun, then the plural encompasses absolutely all aspects and forms of the named noun. In essence, what this means is that whilst all angels have specific duties, as ordained by Allāh Almighty, they will all conform to this ruling, and they will all - without exception - be engaged in the task of continuously showering the Prophet ﷺ with blessings. No angel, therefore, has ever or will ever be exempt from this duty. (p. 9. *Blessings & Salutations on the Best of Creation*. Muhammad Nawaz Siddiqui

3.4. Who are superior; humans or angels?

There is a long-standing argument whether humans are superior in the eyes of Allāh or angels. Overall, it seems most of the Ahl al-Sunna have accepted that humans are superior. Here is a summary of the two sides of the argument:

3.4.1. *Humans are superior.*

- Allāh ordered the angels to bow to Ādam (peace be upon him). This indicates that the messengers are superior, since the inferior bow to the superior.

- Allāh taught Ādam the names of all things (2: 31). The story indicates that Allāh intended to highlight the superiority of man over angels, since he possessed more knowledge.

- In the Qur'ān, Allāh states:

> 'Indeed Allāh chose Ādam, Nūh, the family of Ibrāhīm and the family of Imrān over the worlds (*Ālamīn*).' (3:33)

This shows that messengers are better than angels, since the angels are part of the worlds (*Ālamīn*).

3.4.2. *Angels are superior.*

Those who argue that angels are better do so on the following grounds:

- The Mu'tazila[67], philosophers and some Ashā'ira have suggested that

Hazarvi).

67 The term Mu'tazila refers to an early Islamic school of thought that flourished in Basra and Baghdad in the first few centuries of Islām. The origins of the Mu'tazila can be traced back to Wāsil ibn Atā (d.131), who parted from the company of Hasan

angels are superior to men because they are pure spirits, free from lust and anger.[68]

In response to this, the Ahl al-Sunna say that angels are totally subservient, and could not perform sin even if they wanted to. Allāma Sa'd al-Dīn Taftazānī (d. 793/1390) explains:

> 'Man achieves virtues and perfection in knowledge and practice in spite of such hindrances and impediments such as lust and anger and the recurrence of necessary wants which diverts his attention from acquiring the perfections of life. There is no doubt that religious service and acquiring perfections, when done in spite of preoccupations, are more difficult and display further sincerity; so man is more excellent.'[69]

- Some have argued that angels are better because the prophets actually learned from the angels and benefited from them. Allāh says in the Qur'ān:

> 'He (the Prophet) has been taught by the one mighty in power (Jibrā'īl).' (53:5)

And the teacher is better than the student.

In refutation of this, Taftazānī says that in essence it was Allāh teaching the prophets; the angels were merely intermediaries passing on His message.

- The third argument is that there are many places in the Qur'ān where

---

al-Basrī. Amongst their beliefs is that when a Muslim commits a major sin, then he is neither a believer nor infidel.

68 pp. 177-178. *Sharh al-Aqā'id al-Nasfiyya*. Allāma Sa'd al-Dīn al-Taftazānī.

69 Ibid. For example, when two teenagers are given an illegal opportunity to drive a sports car – one knows how to drive and the other does not know at all – then the former deserves more congratulations for his restraint. Similarly, humans are better because they can refrain from sins when they have the choice to indulge in it.

the angels are mentioned first before the prophets in a sentence. For example:

> 'Each one believes in Allāh, His angels, and His messengers...' (2:285)

Their being mentioned first is only – according to the argument – because they are better in honour and dignity.

The answer to this is that they are mentioned first because their existence was prior to that of man. Also, believing in them is more of a mystery and so belief in them is emphasised more.

However there can be no doubt that some angels hold a very special rank and perform some important duties of Allāh, like holding the *Arsh* of Allāh and serving the prophets. With this in mind, Allāma Sa'd al-Dīn Taftazānī orders the superiority rankings in the following manner.

a. The messengers from the men.

b. The messengers from the angels (such as Jibrā'īl).

c. Ordinary (believing) men.

d. Ordinary angels.[70]

3.5. Conclusion.

There are a few points worthy of mention regarding belief in angels. Firstly, in Sūrah Baqara, the first description of a pious believer is one 'who believes in the unseen' (2: 3). Our belief in angels reflects the strength of our faith; that we believe in something we cannot see, feel or

---

70 p. 176. *Sharh al-Aqā'id al-Nasfiyya*. Allāma Sa'd al-Dīn al-Taftazānī.

hear. The fact that Allāh and His Messenger informed us that they exist is sufficient for us to wholeheartedly believe in them.

Secondly, in essence, it is Allāh who performs all of the angelic duties such as sending the rain and taking the souls, but He himself ascribes these acts to His angels. This is the biggest indication that though Allāh has control of everything, He can ascribe certain acts to His creation. As Abdul Hakim Murad observed:

> 'The Burāq[71] exists to indicate the nature of the *Asbāb*. Nothing is more indicative of God than His conventions.'

Thirdly, the Muslims believe that the Prophet ﷺ is *Nūr* (light), as proven from the Holy Qur'ān.[72] Sceptics say that it is impossible for the Prophet to be *Nūr* and *Bashar* (human) simultaneously. He is either one or the other. In response, we say that this maxim is not proven. Jibrā'īl (peace be upon him) is an angel and thus created from light. But he appeared in the form of a man without anyone knowing (as mentioned in the famous *Hadīth Jibrā'īl*). Likewise, Iblīs was created from fire. But he too appeared in the form of a man without Abū Huraira ؓ knowing.[73]

---

71 This is the animal which the Prophet embarked on for the miraculous Night Journey from Makka to Jerusalem.

72 There are two verses which prove that the Prophet is Nūr: (a)'O Prophet! Verily, We have sent you as witness, and a bearer of glad tidings, and a warner. And as one who invites to Allāh by His Leave, and as a lamp, a provider of light.' (33:45-6) The verse describes Prophet as (i) Sirāj (Lamp). Metaphors are used to describe an object with another for its known quality. 'Zaid is a lion' denotes his bravery because lions are known primarily for their bravery. The Prophet (peace and blessings of Allāh be upon him) is described as Sirāj because he primarily provides light just like a lamp does (ii) Munīr (Provider of light). One can only be a provider of light if one possesses it himself. A teacher can only teach if he has knowledge to disperse. The Prophet (peace and blessings of Allāh be upon him) can only provide light if he possesses it in the first place. (b)'There has come to you from Allāh a light and a clear Book.' (5: 15)Most classical *Tafsīrs* of the Qur'ān state that the 'light' refers to the Prophet (peace and blessings of Allāh be upon him) and 'a clear book' refers to the Holy Qur'ān. Examples are *Tafsīr ibn Jarīr Tabarī, Tafsīr Khāzin, Tafsīr Kabīr, Tafsīr Mu'ālam Tanzīl, Tafsīr Rūh al-Bayān, Tafsīr Rūh al-Ma'ānī* and *Tafsīr Sāwī ala Jalālain.*

73 *Sahīh al-Bukhārī: Book of Representation (Wikāla).*

Chapter Four

Belief in the Divine Scriptures

4.0. The Divine Scriptures - Introduction.

It is an essential part of our faith to believe that Allāh Almighty sent down divine scriptures to mankind to guide them. The Qur'ān states:

> 'Say (O people): We believe in Allāh and that which has been revealed to us...'(2: 136)

We must believe that each divine book is the word of Allāh. From the Qur'ān and Sunna, we know a handful of the names of these divine scriptures and which messenger they were revealed to. The exact number of divine scriptures and their names is in the knowledge of Allāh, but we must believe in all of them.

4.1. The main, Divine Scriptures.

There are four, main divine books. They are:

1. The Qur'ān, revealed to Prophet Muhammad ﷺ.

2. The Injīl, revealed to Īsā (peace be upon him).

3. The Torāh, revealed to Mūsā (peace be upon him).

4. The Zabūr, revealed to Dāwūd (peace be upon him).

Smaller works were given to certain messengers such as Ibrāhīm and Ādam (peace be upon them). These works are referred to as *Sahīfas*.[74]

4.2. The protection and preservation of the Divine Scriptures.

We have been informed by Allāh that the previous scriptures were altered. The Qur'ān states that:

> 'Then woe to those who write the Book with their own hands and then say: "This is from Allāh" in order to purchase it with a little price. Woe to them for what their hands have written and woe to them for that which they have earned.' (2: 79)
>
> 'From the Jews are those who altered the words from its [correct] places...' (4:46)

The followers of the previous scriptures indulged in concealment, fabrication and distortion. For example, one of the things they hid was the appearance of Muhammad ﷺ, something which was certainly mentioned in their scriptures.

The previous divine scriptures suffered from alteration and change for two reasons:

a. Allāh left the responsibility to preserve them in the hands of the corresponding messengers and their followers.

74 p. 146. *al-Aqīda al-Hasana (al-Mar'ūf bi) Aqā'id al-Islām*. Hazrat Shāh Walī Allāh Muhaddith Delhvī.

b. The messengers and their followers did not always memorise the texts they were given.

The Qur'ān is immune from such changes and alterations. Because the Qur'ān was revealed as the last word of Allāh to mankind, and because it was meant to be a source of guidance until the Day of Judgement, Allāh himself took on the responsibility to preserve it. The Qur'ān states:

> 'Verily we revealed the Remembrance (i.e. the Qur'ān) and verily We are its protectors.' (15:9)

The Qur'ān's preservation was helped by the fact that it was made easy to memorise; for the Prophet ﷺ and his followers. Allāh says:

> 'Rather it is clear signs in the chests of those who have been given knowledge.' (29:49)

Also, Allāh says:

> 'We have made the Quran easy for remembrance, so is there anyone that will remember?' (54:17)

Additionally, this means that the Qur'ān – because it is the final word of Allāh – has abrogated all previous scriptures.

4.3. The names of the Qur'ān.

Principally, the Qur'ān is known by four other names:

i. *al-Kitāb* (The Book).

ii. *al-Furqān* (The Standard).

iii. *al-Zikr* (The Remembrance).

iv. *al-Tanzil* (The Revelation).

There are countless other descriptive names of the Qur'ān too.[75]

4.4. The gathering of the Qur'ān.

Muslims believe that the gathering and compilation of the Qur'ān was the work of Allāh in reality:

> 'Indeed it is upon us to gather it and recite it.' (75:17)

Through the Prophet's ﷺ authority and guidance, it is possible to identify three key stages in the gathering of the Qur'ān.

4.4.1. Stage One; During the Prophet's lifetime.

Over a period of twenty-three years, the Qur'ān was revealed part by part, according to need and circumstances. Secure steps were taken to ensure it was memorised and recorded accurately. For example;

- When a verse was revealed, the Prophet ﷺ himself would memorise it and then instruct his Companions to memorise it too. He would also inform them which Sūrah the verses belonged to.[76] Zaid ibn Thābit ؓ was one of the regular scribes in Madina because he was situated near the Prophet's mosque. Once the revelation was recorded the scribe would read it back to the Prophet, who would then certify it. Other famous Companions who were entrusted with learning the Qur'ān include Abd Allāh ibn Mas'ūd, Ubayy Ibn Ka'b, Mu'āz ibn Jabal, Ā'isha,

75 Muhammad Rafiq Choudary lists the descriptive names of the Qur'ān (in *An interview with the Qur'ān*, 1980) which include *Rahma, Hikma, Hudā, Mubīn, Karīm, Kalām, Burhān, Nūr, Shifā, Maw'iza, Mubārak, Hakīm, Musaddiq, Ahsan al-Hadīth, Ilm, Haqq, Tazkira, Bushrā, Azīm, Nazīr* and *Balāgh*.

76 p. 152. *al-Aqīda al-Hasana (al-Mar'ūf bi) Aqā'id al-Islām*. Hazrat Shāh Walī Allāh Muhaddith Delhvī.

Hafsa and Umm Salma (may Allāh be pleased with them).

- The Prophet ﷺ would recite the verses in Salāh as well as during his speeches.

- He would highlight the superior reward for learning, memorising and teaching the Holy Qur'ān. In one Hadīth, he said:

> 'The best of you is the one who learns the Qur'ān and then teaches others.'[77]

- Jibrā'īl (peace be upon him) would appear every Ramadān to listen to and recite the Qur'ān with the Prophet ﷺ. In his last Ramadān on earth, the Prophet ﷺ revised the Qur'ān with him twice.[78]

- The Qur'ān was written on papers, parchments, the shoulder blades of sheep and camels, sheets of stone, leather and palm branches stripped of their leaves.[79]

- Imām Muslim (d. 261/874) narrates in his *Sahīh* that the Prophet did not order his own sayings to be recorded on paper for a short period of time.[80] This meant that the Muslims were not allowed to record the revelations of the Qur'ān and the Hadīth of the Prophet in the same place, in order to avoid confusion between the two.

- One important fact to remember is that the ordering of the verses and chapters actually took place in the Prophet's time, contrary to the belief of certain Western Qur'ān scholars such as Goddard.[81]

---

77 *Sahīh al-Bukhārī*. Book; the Superiority of the Qur'ān. Chapter, 'the best of you is the one who learns the Qur'ān and then teaches others.' Hadīth no. 4639.
78 *Sahīh al-Bukhārī*, Book; the Superiority of the Qur'ān, Hadīth no. 4613.
79 p. 37. Vol. I. Introduction to *Tafsīr al-Qurtubī.*
80 *Sahīh Muslim*. Book of Zuhd wa Raqā'iq. Chapter, Authenticity in reporting and the principle of writing the Hadīth. Hadīth no. 5326.
81 p. 37. *Christians and Muslims from Double Standards to Mutual Understanding*. Goddard, H.

4.4.2. Stage Two; The Caliphate of Abū Bakr.

The Qur'ān in written form was present in the time of the Prophet ﷺ on scattered papers but was not in one, formal document. One reason why this did not happen is because the revelation was a continual process, lasting twenty-three years. The task to gather it as such fell on Abū Bakr ؓ.

Abū Bakr ؓ had to deal with two major problems during his Caliphate; the Muslims who would not pay Zakāh and the *Fitna* of false prophets. Musailma Kazzāb was one such culprit, and the Muslims defeated him in the Battle of Yamāma.

After the Battle of Yamāma (in the eleventh year of Hijrah), many Huffāz (memorisers of the Qur'ān) were martyred. Umar petitioned Abū Bakr to commission the gathering of the Qur'ān into a single book to preserve it from being lost. After initial reservations, Abū Bakr instructed Zaid ibn Thābit ؓ to gather the Qur'ān.[82]

Zaid ibn Thābit ؓ duly obliged and set about accomplishing this great task. He began by contacting the people who had portions of the Qur'ān. He was also ordered along with Umar to sit on the door step of the Mosque and collect the Qur'ān from those people who came to them with two witnesses to prove the validity of their claim. This task lasted almost a year and when it was completed the Companions expressed their admiration and appreciation.

Each Sūrah was written separately on an individual paper.

The final work remained in the hands of Abū Bakr, and was then passed on to Umar and then Hafsa bint al-Fārūq (may Allāh be pleased with

---

82 *Sahīh al-Bukhārī*. Book, the Tafsīr of the Qur'ān. Chapter, the saying of Allāh: 'Verily from Allāh has come to you a Prophet...' Hadīth no. 4311.

her).[83] However, at this moment in time, a copy was not distributed to the Muslim lands.

4.4.3. Stage Three; The Caliphate of Uthmān.

The third stage of the gathering of the Qur'ān occurred in the time of Uthmān ﷺ. The Muslims had slowly advanced their frontiers and more and more people had accepted Islām. Due to this expansion, the Qur'ān's recitation was becoming diverse and it was being recited in different dialects. This reached an alarming stage where people began to dispute as to which was the correct dialect.[84]

Uthmān ﷺ gathered all the papers into one book form in the Quraishī dialect. This was completed in the twenty-fifth year of Hijrah.[85] Copies were sent to the different Muslim lands. By taking the necessary steps in properly compiling the Qur'ān into a book, in one dialect, Uthmān ﷺ had resolved any disputes and had prepared a standard copy for Muslims everywhere. It was not incumbent upon the Muslims to learn all the different modes of recitation of the Qur'ān. Therefore to erase any dispute or doubt, these steps were taken.

According to Hārūn ibn Mūsā, it was Yahyā ibn Ma'mar al-Basrī (d. 89/707) who was the first to add the dots (to the letters) on the Holy Qur'an.[86]

---

83 p. 152. *al-Aqīda al-Hasana (al-Mar'ūf bi) Aqā'id al-Islām*. Hazrat Shāh Walī Allāh Muhaddith Delhvī.

84 pp. 38-9. Vol. I. *Tafsīr al-Qurtubī.* The various recitations of the Qur'ān did not arise after the Prophet passed away, but in fact was something that had been present in his time. Abd Allāh Ibn Abbās reports: Allāh's Apostle said: 'Gabriel recited the Qur'ān to me in one way. Then I requested him (to read it in another way), and continued asking him to recite it in other ways, and he recited it in several ways till he ultimately recited it in seven different ways.' (*Sahīh al-Bukhārī*, (Vol VI, book 61, no: 513), translated by Dr.Mohsin Khān, Kāzī Publications, Pakistan, 1986). One should not assume that the different dialects meant a different meaning.

85 p. XXVIII. Introduction to *Kanzul Imān*. Maulana Shāh Ahmad Razā Khān. English translation by Professor Shāh Farīd al-Haque.

86 p. 192. *Tahzīb al-Tahzīb*, Ibn Hajar al-Asqalānī.

4.5. Objections from the Orientalists on the Qur'ān.[87]

Western scholars for centuries have attempted to confuse and misguide Muslims by raising objections about the Qur'ān. Their attempts have been shallow, inaccurate and fruitless. The Qur'ān asserts that it is the word of God and challenges those who suggest otherwise to replicate it. Allāh says:

> 'Say (O Messenger) if all mankind and the jinn would come together to produce the like of this Qur'ān, they could not produce its like even if they exerted all their strength in aiding one another.' (17:88)

Just like the Arabs before them, the Orientalists have failed in trying to match the Qur'ān in any aspect.

Here are some of their key objections on the Qur'ān.

4.5.1. *'The Qur'ān is not the Word of God.'*

The majority of Western scholars have never accepted the Qur'ān as the word of Allāh. The same allegation was made by the Arab polytheists. Upon hearing the glorious revelation, the Meccan Pagans proclaimed:

> 'This revelation is nothing but a lie which he (Muhammad) has forged and others have helped at it.' (25:4)

Orientalists like Alois Sprenger, William Muir, Theodor Noldeke, Ignas Goldziher, and W. Wellhausen have repeated the same objection. Their

---

87 Professor Abd al-Qādir Sayyid Abd al-Raūf (from the Department of Theology, al-Azhar University) quotes Professor Abd al-Ghafūr Azīz in his definition of Orientalism: '[Orientalism is] the study conducted by westerners on the doctrine of the Islamic east, its civilization, language, morals, history, norms and habits and so on. A person who occupies himself with such studies is called a *Mustashriq*' (*Darāsāt fi al-Tabshīr wa al-Istishrāq*).

works have been further developed and summarised by 'scholars' like Richard Bell and his student Montgomery Watt.

Our Response:

- Allāh ensured that the Prophet ﷺ was not seen to read and write in public. The precise reason for this was so no one could claim that Muhammad wrote the Qur'ān himself, or he learnt it from others. The Qur'ān states:

> 'And you were not used to reading any book before this nor to writing with your right hand; otherwise the followers of falsehood would have had doubt.' (29:48)

Even Montgomery Watt admits:

> 'The probability is that Muhammad could read and write sufficiently for business purposes, but it seems that he had not read any (religious) scriptures.'[88]

- The enemies of the Prophet ﷺ were experts in Arabic. If the Qur'ān was man-written, why did they display marvel at its eloquence and why could they not produce words like it? [89]

- Furthermore, we find in the Holy Qur'ān scientific facts which have

---

88 p. 26. *'Muhammad's Mecca'* in *Religion in pre-Islamic Arabia.* Watt, W.M.

89 When Walīd ibn Mughīra, the uncle of Abū Jahl, heard the Qur'ān he told his tribe; 'By God I have just heard from Muhammad (peace be upon him) what is not the speech of a human or a jinn, for it is abundantly sweet.' (p. 163. *al-Shifā.* Qādī Iyādh (d. 544/1149).
It was a practice during the time of the Prophet (peace and blessings of Allāh be upon him) that whenever someone wrote a poem that was matchless in eloquence and literal beauty, the poem would be hung on the wall of the Ka'ba for everyone to admire. Labīd ibn Rabiyah, a master of literature at that time, had been bestowed this honour. However, when Sūrah Baqarah was revealed it was also hung on the wall of Ka'ba beside the poem of Labīd. Labīd, who was a polytheist at the time, went to inspect it and he was so amazed by it that he proclaimed: 'This is such work that no one has the power to produce it except he who receives revelation!'

been proven as truthful only in the last one hundred years. How could the Prophet ﷺ, living in the sixth century;

-Describe the evolution of the embryo inside the uterus with utmost accuracy, as we find it in modern science? (22:5)

-Describe the concept of reproduction in the plant kingdom, outlining sexual and asexual reproduction? (36:36)

-Be aware that the density of air decreases with altitude so that breathing becomes difficult? (6:125)

-Identify that all living things are made from water? (21:30)

The only way the Qur'ān could contain such information is if it was written by the Creator of all that exists, Allāh Almighty.

4.5.2. *'Only four Companions had memorised the Qur'ān.'*

The Orientalists claim that during the Prophet's lifetime – according to the Hadīth recorded by Imām al-Bukhārī – only four people memorised the Qur'ān; Abū al-Dardā, Mu'āz ibn Jabal, Zaid ibn Thābit and Abū Zaid.

Our Response:

This objection stems from a lack of understanding of Arabic. The Hadīth being referred to is the saying of Anas ibn Mālik ﷺ who said:

مات النبي صلي الله عليه و سلم و لم يجمع
القران غير أربعة أبو الدرداء و معاذ بن جبل و
زيد بن ثابت و أبو زيد

'The Prophet ﷺ passed away in the state that no one gathered (*Yajma'*) the Qur'ān except four: Abū al-Dardā, Mu'āz ibn Jabal, Zaid ibn Thābit and Abū Zaid.' [90]

The word is no one *gathered* (*Yajma'*) the Qur'ān, in written form. It does not refer to *memorising* the Qur'ān, which is *Hifz* in Arabic. As it has been mentioned, countless Companions memorised the Qur'ān. In the Battle of Yamāma, it is reported that seven hundred *Companions* who had memorised the Qur'ān were martyred.[91] So how can it be said that only four had memorised the Qur'ān? [92]

Also, Abd Allāh ibn Mas'ūd's name is not mentioned in the above four though it is well known that he was a Hāfiz. In fact, the Prophet actually instructed Muslims to learn the Qur'ān from him.[93] Would the Prophet have told his Companions to learn the Qur'ān from him if he ﷺ knew that he did not know it?

4.5.3. *'Uthmān burnt copies of the Qur'ān.'*

Noldeke[94] claims that when Uthmān ﷺ compiled the Qur'ān into one standard copy, he had the others burnt to hide the fact that there were huge discrepancies.

---

90 *Sahīh al-Bukhārī*. Book; the Superiority of the Qur'ān, Chapter, the reciters from the Companions, Hadīth no. 4620.

91 p. XV. Introduction to *Kanzul Imān*. Maulāna Shāh Ahmad Razā Khān. English translation by Professor Shāh Farid al-Haque. See also Introduction to *Tafsīr al-Qurtubī*. p. 37. Vol. I.

92 Moreover, it should be mentioned that the Arabs were known for their great memory and they preferred to secure facts by heart rather than writing it down. Zwettler acknowledges:
'In the ancient times, when writing was scarcely used, memory and oral transmission was exercised and strengthened to a degree now almost unknown.' (p.14. *The Oral Tradition of Classical Arabic Poetry*).

93 *Sahīh al-Bukhārī*. Book of Superiorities. Chapter; the superiority of Sālim Maulā Abū Huzaifa. Hadīth no. 3475.

94 pp. 88-90, vol. I. '*Provenance and Transmission*' in *The Koran, Critical concepts in Islamic Studies*, Noldeke, T.

Our Response:

Certainly, we agree that Uthmān ﷺ did burn copies of the Qur'ān, but the reason was not because he wanted to hide the huge discrepancies. Rather, it was done with the intention of standardising the *dialects*. The meaning and the message of the Qur'ān was not at all distorted.

4.6. Conclusion.

Orientalism is a nuisance to Muslims, but not a threat. Because we wholly believe that Islām is the only true religion and that the Qur'ān is the unchanged words of Allāh, we are happy for non-Muslims to inspect, study and scrutinise our religion.

However, it is sad to see that perhaps 80% of Islamic literature produced in the Indian Sub-Continent is geared towards internal divisions in Islām (Wahhābism, Deobandism, Salafism, Qādiānism, Shi'ism) and not towards the external threat of Orientalism. Academic effort should also be focussed on quashing the misconceptions propagated by the Orientalists.

Chapter Five

Belief in Messengers

5.0. Messengers - Introduction.

Allāh created prophets and messengers to deliver and preach the message of Islām to mankind. These figures play a crucial link between Allāh and His servants.[95] Without them, we have no real means of knowing Allāh, what He has ordered us to do and what He has asked us to refrain from.

Therefore it is compulsory upon us to believe that Allāh has sent prophets and messengers throughout the history of mankind. They are the chosen, pious servants of Allāh entrusted with preaching His word on earth.

5.1. The definition of *Nabī* and *Rasūl*.

Rasūl:

'A free male who has been given revelation (*Wahy*) in the form of a Sharī'ah from Allāh and has been ordered to preach it.' [96]

---

95 p. 132. *Sharh al-Aqā'id al-Nasfiyya*. Allāma Sa'd al-Dīn al-Taftazānī.
96 p. 16. Ibid.

Nabī:

'A free male who has been chosen by Allāh and has been ordered to preach the Sharī'ah given to a previous Rasūl.'

In essence, there is only a slight difference between a Nabī and Rasūl. Both are chosen men of Allāh and both are supported with miracles. But a Rasūl is given a fresh Sharī'ah and has been ordered to teach mankind this message, whereas a Nabī simply implements a previous Sharī'ah. So every Rasūl is a Nabī, but not vice versa.

Note that only males can become prophets and messengers. Allāh has never sent a female prophet.[97] Allāh states:

> 'And We did not send before you (O Muhammad) except *men* whom We inspired...' (21: 7).

5.2. The attributes of messengers.

5.2.1. What is necessary for them.

In short, all prophets and messengers are marked with praiseworthy characteristics to reflect their divine role and their exalted relation with Allāh Almighty – traits such as tolerance, justness, truthfulness, piety and nobility.

Specifically, the scholars have identified four attributes that all prophets and messengers possess.[98]

---

97 On the basis that Maryam (peace be upon her) received instructions from Jibrā'īl, some Orientalists (and unfortunately some Muslims) have assumed that women can become prophets. The scholars all agree unanimously that this does not at all prove she was a prophet; rather she was a pious servant of Allāh who was granted *Karāmats* (miracles to beings other than prophets and messengers) from Allāh.

98 pp. 63-65. *Sharh al-Risāla al-Nāfi'a wa al-Hujaj al-Qāti'a*. Sheikh Muhammad Abd al-Latīf

5.2.1.1 *Sidq* (Truthfulness).

In other words, they have never spoken except the truth, before official revelation and after. If – God forbid – they could lie, then people would have no means of knowing whether the message of Islām they teach is truthful or not. The task of the prophets is to draw people towards them, not repel them. An evil trait such as lying would only drive people away.[99]

5.2.1.2 *Fitāna* (Intelligence).

In order to successfully preach the message of Islām and repel likely objections and stubbornness, all prophets are marked with wisdom and unparalleled intellect.

For example, when Ibrāhīm preached the oneness of Allāh to Nimrūd, he introduced Allāh as the one 'Who gives life and death' (2: 258). Nimrūd dismissed this and brought two people in front of Ibrāhīm; one was a prisoner who was about to be executed and one was an innocent, free man. He killed the innocent man and granted freedom to the prisoner and then remarked: 'I can cause life and death [too]' (2: 258). Ibrāhīm then showed his intelligence by saying to Nimrūd:

> 'Verily! Allāh causes the sun to rise from the east; then cause it to rise from the west.'

Upon this, Nimrūd was left speechless (2: 258).

Sālih al-Farfūr (d. 1407/1986).

99 In a Hadīth recorded by Abū Dāwūd in his *Sunan*, Abd Allāh ibn Umar said: 'I intended to write everything I heard from the Prophet (peace and blessings of Allāh be upon him) to memorise, but Quraish stopped me. They said: 'Do you want to write *everything* you hear from the Messenger of Allāh when he is a man who talks in content and in anger?' So I stopped writing. I later mentioned this case to the Prophet (peace and blessings of Allāh be upon him). He pointed to his lips and said: 'Do write. By Allāh! Nothing has emitted [from these lips] except the truth!' (Hadīth no. 3161). This Hadīth is clear proof that the Prophet could only speak the truth.

5.2.1.3 *Tablīgh mā Umirū bi hī* (to preach what they have been ordered to).

The prophets and messengers must all fully convey the message of Islām, without distortion. Allāh states:

> '(O Muhammad!) Your duty is to only convey the clear message.' (16: 82)

If – hypothetically speaking – they were to hide anything from their preaching, then this would cause doubt in their prophet-hood and it would be a reason for the people to reject their message.

5.2.1.4. *Amāna* (Trustworthiness).

What this means is that outwardly and inwardly, they are immune from things that Allāh has prohibited, before the official revelation and after. This is also called *Isma* (immunity from sin).

The reason for this is simple; we have been ordered unequivocally to follow the footsteps of the prophets (3:31 & 4:59). If they can commit sin and show disobedience to Allāh, then this means – as the followers – this is permissible for us too. Moreover it would not be befitting to Allāh's lofty status to choose men for His mission who are sinful and disobedient.

5.2.1.4.1. Evidence to support the immunity of prophets from sin.

a. The Qur'ān highlights the immunity of prophets from sin in several places. For example, the Devil told Allāh:

> 'I shall mislead them all. Except Your chosen (guided) slaves

amongst them' (15: 40).

In other words, this is an admission from the Devil that he cannot mislead the chosen servants of Allāh. And of all of Allāh's servants, no one is closer to Him than His prophets.

b. The Prophet ﷺ himself said:

> 'There is no one from amongst you except that he has been allocated a jinn (to entice evil) and an angel (to encourage good).' The Companions asked: 'Even you, O Prophet of Allāh?' He replied: 'Even me. But Allāh assisted me so the jinn only orders me to perform good.'[100]

c. The Qur'ān orders Muslims not to accept the news of wrongdoers at face level but to further investigate the validity of the news. Allāh says:

> 'O those who believe! If a sinner comes to you (*Fāsiq*) with news, then investigate...' (49: 6).

The purpose of a prophet is to give important news to the people about Allāh. In fact, the word *Nabī* in Arabic means 'deliverer of important news'. If prophets were allowed to sin, then according to the Qur'ān their reports should not be accepted at face level. Allāma Taftazānī (d. 793/1390) writes:

> '...Indeed the prophets are immune (*Ma'sūm*) from falsity, especially in what is connected with the commanding of laws and the conveying of judgements and the guidance of people.'[101]

100 *Musnad Ahmad.* The Musnad of Abd Allāh ibn Mas'ūd, Hadīth no. 3466.
101 p. 139. *Sharh al-Aqā'id al-Nasfiyya.* Allāma Sa'd al-Dīn al-Taftazānī.

5.2.1.4.2. Objections.

In the Qur'ān and Sunna, there are cases where it seems that prophets and messengers did make mistakes. Some argue that this is a reason to suggest that prophets and messengers are not necessarily immune from sins. For example:

- Ādam (peace be upon him) ate the forbidden fruit, and as a result he was punished by Allāh by being ousted from Paradise (2:36).

- Ibrāhīm (peace be upon him) reportedly lied on three occasions (i) when his people invited him to the fair, he said: 'I am sick' (ii) he destroyed the idols but when he was asked about it, he said: 'The big idol did it' (iii) speaking about his wife, he said: 'This is my sister.'

- The Prophet ﷺ made mistakes in leading the Prayers on certain occasions. This suggests he is fallible.

- Mūsā (peace be upon him) struck a man who then died.

5.2.1.4.3. Answers.

Ādam (peace be upon him):

- With regards to the 'original sin,' we must focus on the statement Allāh delivered to the angels when He was about to create Ādam:

> 'And remember (O Prophet) when your Lord said to the angels: 'Indeed I am going to make a vicegerent on *earth* [my italics]...' (2: 30)

Clearly, Allāh's intention was always to make man a *Khalīfa* on earth and not in heaven. So the eating of the fruit was not the reason why he was ousted from paradise; man was always destined to live on earth.

Also, a sin is only considered as such when there is deliberate intent behind it. With Ādam (peace be upon him), no such intent is found and in fact Allāh makes this clear Himself:

> 'And indeed We made a covenant with Ādam before, but he forgot, and We found on his part no firm intent [of sin].' (20:115)

Indeed, the Sufi saints mention that Ādam (peace be upon him) had to leave paradise because the souls of the infidels and sinners were in his loins. Due to them being unworthy of paradise, Allāh ordered Ādam to leave until the Day of Judgement, when only the deserved would re-enter paradise. [102]

Ibrāhīm (peace be upon him):

- Under compulsion and when one fears for his life, then speaking lies is not a sin. In fact saying the words of disbelief (as long as the heart remains firm with faith) is permitted (16: 106). When Ibrāhīm (peace be upon him) said about his wife 'this is my sister' he was worried that the tyrannical king would snatch her away.[103] Also, he could have meant 'this is my sister in religion.'[104]

  Secondly, when he was asked whether he broke all the idols, (to which he replied 'the big one did it'), he was highlighting the foolishness and shallowness of their beliefs. The people thought the idols were worthy of worship and could help them in worldly and heavenly affairs. Ibrāhīm (peace be upon him) showed them that the idols could not

---

102 p. 469. *The Obliteration of Falsehood (Jā al-Haqq).* Mufti Ahmad Yaar Khan (English Translation by Moulana Omar Dawood Qadri). Mufti Khan also suggests that the Devil was responsible for this incident, not Ādam. Iblīs took an oath using Allāh's name and Ādam assumed that anyone taking such an oath must be truthful.

103 p. 471. *The Obliteration of Falsehood (Jā al-Haqq).* Mufti Ahmad Yaar Khan (English Translation by Moulana Omar Dawood Qadri).

104 The Qur'ān has mentioned Akhū (brother) to mean brother in religion, not brother in relation. It states in Sūrah Swād: 'This, my brother (in religion), has ninety-nine ewes, while I only have one ewe.' (38:23).

even protect themselves.

Thirdly, when Ibrāhīm (peace be upon him) said to his people that he was ill (*Saqīm*), it could have meant that 'watching you worship idols other than Allāh is making me sick.'[105]

In short, these statements from Ibrāhīm (peace be upon him) were *seemingly* lies in our eyes, but not in the sights of Allāh. If these 'lies' were deliberate and malice, then surely Allāh would have reproached his messenger. Instead, we find that Allāh gave him the title of *Khalīl* (close friend) (4: 125) and said that 'We bestowed Ibrāhīm guidance' (21:51).

Prophet Muhammad ﷺ:

- The Prophet ﷺ did certainly read Salāh incorrectly on certain occasions.[106] But this was purely to teach his followers what to do when they are forgetful in prayers. In other words, it was a deliberate mistake for our sake.[107] If the Prophet ﷺ never performed a delayed Salāh (*Qadhā*) or never made a mistake in Salāh, then how would we ever know what to do in similar circumstances? The Prophet ﷺ epitomised this issue when he reportedly said: 'I do not forget but I am made to forget.'[108]

105 p. 298. vol. VI. *Lisān al-Arab*. Ibn Manzūr (d.711/1311).

106 Imām al-Bukhārī reports from Abū Huraira (may Allāh be pleased with him) that he once performed two Rak'ats with the Companions and then performed Salām. A Companion called Zūl Yadain asked: 'O Mẹssenger of Allāh! Has Salāh now become shorter or did you forget?' The Prophet (peace and blessings of Allāh be upon him) asked the Companions if he had indeed read only two and they confirmed this. So he stood up, performed two more and then performed Sajda Sahv (the prostration of forgetfulness) at the end. *Sahīh al-Bukhārī*. Book of Azān. Hadīth no. 673.

107 p. 64. *Sharh al-Risāla al-Nāfi'a wa al-Hujaj al-Qāti'a*. Sheikh Muhammad Abd al-Latīf Sālih al-Farfūr (d. 1407/1986).

108 p. 342. *al-Shifā*. Qādī Iyādh.

Mūsā (peace be upon him):

- Mūsā had no intention of killing anyone. Rather, he wished to free the Jew from the unfair Egyptian. When the Egyptian did not free him, he struck him to separate them. The man could not bear the might of a prophet and died. This therefore does not count as murder, which is a crime that requires deliberate intent. [109]

Conclusion.

Overall, the Ahl al-Sunna hold all the prophets and messengers in highest regard and do not contemplate uttering even the smallest remark which may de-rank their lofty status. The lapses that have been reported from the Qur'ān and Sunna (such as Ādam's eating of the forbidden fruit) are not something we should dwell on. Our position is clearly explained in *Bahār Sharī'at*:

> 'Any mention of the lapses on the part of the prophets if any, except those mentioned in the Holy Qur'ān and Hadīth is a serious taboo. No one should ever depreciate a misdemeanour of the prophets. It is only Allāh, the All-Powerful, who can mete out to his prophets any treatment he thinks fit for them. No one else has this prerogative...Even a small lapse on the part of a prophet is equal to thousands of acts of wisdom of an ordinary person. [110]

The scholars mention a very important phrase which helps us to understand this issue.

---

109 p. 475. *The Obliteration of Falsehood (Jā al-Haqq)*. Mufti Ahmad Yaar Khan (English Translation by Moulana Omar Dawood Qadri).

110 p 24. *Islam: The Basic Articles of Faith, according to the Beliefs of the Ahl Sunna wa al-Jāma'a; A Modern English Translation of Bahar-e-Shariat*. Part One.

حسنات الابرار سيأت المقربين

'The good actions of the pious are the sins of the [chosen] close servants.'[111]

What we consider a good action is seen as a lapse by the close servants of Allāh. When we complete the recitation of Sūrah Baqara in a day, then we are pleased with this. The close servants see this as a lapse; it is widely reported that the likes of Imām Shāfi'ī would finish the entire Qur'ān in one night.

5.2.2. What is permissible for them.

The prophets and messengers can be attributed with characteristics that people are usually marked by – like eating, drinking, marriage and human illnesses that do not lead to de-ranking their high status.

As for sleeping, their eyes sleep but their hearts never do. Imām al-Bukhārī (d. 256/869) reports in his *Sahīh* that Ā'isha asked the Prophet whether he slept before performing the Witr prayers (after *Salāh al-Tahajjud*). He replied:

> 'My eyes sleep but my heart does not.'[112]

This is the reason why the Prophet's ablution never broke after sleeping.[113]

---

111 p. 144. *al-Aqīda al-Hasana (al-Mar'ūf bi) Aqā'id al-Islām*. Hazrat Shāh Walī Allāh Muhaddith Delhvī.

112 *Sahīh al-Bukhārī*. Book of Superiorities. Chapter; the Prophet's eyes used to sleep but not his heart, Hadīth no. 3304. In the following Hadīth in the same chapter, Imām al-Bukhārī mentions a report in which the Prophet (peace and blessings of Allāh be upon him) asserts that the same attribute was to be found in all prophets and messengers.

113 p. 66. *Sharh al-Risāla al-Nāfi'a wa al-Hujaj al-Qāti'a*. Sheikh Muhammad Abd al-Latīf Sālih al-Farfūr (d. 1407/1986).

5.2.2. What is impossible for them.

They cannot be attributed with illnesses that will lead to them being seen in a lesser light, such as leprosy, insanity and blindness.

This is why the scholars are very careful when describing the first revelation given to the Prophet ﷺ:

- When Jibrā'īl instructed the Prophet to 'read' in the cave of Hira and he responded ما أنا بقارئ, we interpret this as 'I shall not read' and not 'I cannot read'. Illiteracy is a defect which people see as defamatory.

- When the Prophet ﷺ then returned Sayyida Khadīja (may Allāh be pleased with her), he did not do so in a state of fear, anxiety and thinking that he was possessed by an evil spirit (God forbid). Rather the reaction was from the sheer intensity of the *Wahy* (revelation). Ā'isha (may Allāh be pleased with her) reports that she once saw the Prophet when he was receiving revelation. This was on an extremely cold day but the Prophet was still covered in sweat, due to the intensity of the revelation.[114]

- With regards to Ya'qūb (peace be upon him) and his apparent blindness, the scholars state that this was not permanent and real blindness; rather it was a temporary state that occurred due to his sadness upon the absence of Yūsuf (peace upon him).

5.3. The number of messengers.

It is necessary to believe in all the prophets and messengers that Allāh

114 *Sahīh al-Bukhārī.* Book, the Beginning of the Revelation, Hadīth no. 2. In short, the words of Allāh carry extraordinary weight. The Qur'ān affirms this where we are told that: 'Had We sent down this Qur'ān on a mountain, you would surely have seen it humbling itself and rending asunder from the fear of Allāh' (59: 21).

sent to mankind, the ones we know by name and the ones we do not. The Qur'ān states:

> 'And indeed We have sent messengers before you; some of them We have mentioned to you before (O Muhammad) and some of them We have not mentioned to you' (40:78).

Allāma Sa'd al-Dīn Taftazānī (d. 793/1390) writes that there are some Ahādīth in which the number of prophets Allāh sent was identified. One Hadīth states 124,000 whereas another puts the number at 224,000.[115]

There are twenty-five messengers that Allāh has informed us of in the Holy Qur'ān.[116]

There are four figures in which there are a difference of opinion: Luqmān, Zūl Qarnain, Uzair and Khidr (peace be upon them). Some scholars believe that they are classified as the *Awliyā* (friends of Allāh) rather than his prophets.

5.4. *Mu'jiza* (Miracles).

When Allāh sent prophets and messengers to people, He did so with an undeniable and easily-understandable message. Unfortunately, in each and every generation, some people refused to accept Islām. Sometimes this was because they preferred their own distorted belief system and sometimes they preferred to seek the short-term, worldly gain instead.

Moreover, each and every prophet was tested by their people. They were subject to denial, insult and mockery. In order to convince people

115 p. 138. *Sharh al-Aqā'id al-Nasfiyya*. Allāma Sa'd al-Dīn al-Taftazānī.

116 Ādam, Idrīs, Nūh, Hūd, Sālih, Ibrāhīm, Lūt, Ismā'īl, Ishāq, Ya'qūb, Yūsuf, Ayyūb, Sho'aib, Mūsā, Hārūn, Zūl Kifl, Dāwūd, Sulaimān, Ilyās, al-Yasa', Yūnus, Zakariyya, Yahyā, Isā and the seal of all prophets, Muhammad (may Allāh shower His infinite salutations and blessings upon them all).

that they were indeed the representatives of Allāh, the prophets and messengers were granted miracles that contravened the laws of nature. The purpose behind this *Mu'jiza*s was to produce an extraordinary event that could only happen through the involvement of Allāh.

Allāma Taftazānī defines *Mu'jiza*:

> 'It is something that appears contrary to the customary way of things (*al-Ādat*) at the hands of one who claims the office of prophet, [and it happens] in such a way that those who deny are unable to do the same thing that he does when they compete with him.'[117]

5.4.1. Examples of the Prophet's *Mu'jizas*.

The Prophet ﷺ was granted countless miracles which are almost impossible to encompass. Some of his most famous and widely reported ones – as mentioned in *al-Shifā* – include:

- The Isrā and Mi'rāj (Night Journey and Ascension to Heaven).
- The splitting of the moon.
- The emission of water from his blessed fingers.
- The speech of the tree to the Prophet ﷺ and its walking towards him.
- The tumbling of the 360 idols at the Ka'ba on the mere indication of the Prophet's stick, on the day Makka was conquered.

---

117 p. 134. *Sharh al-Aqā'id al-Nasfiyya*. Allāma Sa'd al-Dīn al-Taftazānī. In *Reliance of the Traveller*, Sheikh Nuh Keller defines a Mu'jiza as 'an event contravening natural laws that appears at the hands of someone who claims to be a prophet and is challenged by those who deny this, such that the deniers are unable to perform the like of it.' (p. 919).

- Curing Qatāda's sight (and in fact making it better than before) when it was directly struck by an arrow during the Battle of Uhud.

- Curing a blind person completely by teaching him a *Du'ā* using himself as a *Wasīla*.[118]

5.5. The Difference between a *Karāma* and a *Mu'jiza*.

Imām Taftazānī explains the subtle difference between a *Mu'jiza* and a *Karāma* when he writes:

> 'The *Karāma*...is the appearance of something that annuls the customary way of things (*al-Ādat*) on the Walī's behalf, but which is not in any way connected with the claim to the prophetic office.'[119]

In other words, a *Mu'jiza* is classified as such when it stems from a prophet. A *Karāma* is something which stems from a saint of Allāh (*Walī*). Both contravene the laws of nature.

Imām Taftazānī asserts that Muslims must also believe that the miracles from the saints of Allāh are true, as many have been mentioned in the Holy Qur'ān and in the Ahādīth. For example:

- Sulaimān's Companion Asaf brought the throne of Bilqīs before the twinkling of an eye, although it was a great distance off (27:40).

- In Maryam's Mihrāb, summer fruits were miraculously found with her in winter, and winter fruits in summer (3: 37).

---

118 pp. 175-190. *al-Shifā*. Qadi Iyādh (d. 544/1149). In fact, *al-Shifā* contains a whole chapter of over eighty pages listing just some of his miracles.

119 p. 145. *Sharh al-Aqā'id al-Nasfiyya*. Allāma Sa'd al-Dīn al-Taftazānī.

- Khālid ibn Walīd ﷺ drank poison without dying. This is because he recited *Bismillāh* before drinking it.[120]

- Whilst on the pulpit in Madina during Friday prayers, Umar ﷺ suddenly shouted 'O Sāriya! The mountain, the mountain!' Sāriya was hundreds of miles away engaged in battle with the enemies. He heard Umar's call and realised it was a warning that the enemies were lurking behind the mountain ready to attack the Muslims.[121]

---

120 p. 147. Ibid.
121 pp. 146-7. Ibid.

Chapter Six

Belief in Messengers II

6. 1. The rank of the prophets and messengers.

There are two aspects explained in the Holy Qur'ān regarding our stance towards the various prophets and messengers Allāh sent; equality and superiority. In terms of prophet-hood, there is no difference between any of the prophets and messengers that Allāh sent. We must believe in all of them equally and no single individual is more of a prophet than another. The Qur'ān states:

> 'We do not make any distinction between anyone from the messengers.' (2:285)

At the same time however, we must accept that some prophets hold more superiority than others;

> 'Those messengers; we gave superiority to some over others. To some of them Allāh spoke (directly)[122] and others He raised several ranks.' (2: 253)

All the scholars agree that in terms of this ranking and superiority,

122 This refers to Mūsā, peace be upon him.

the Prophet ﷺ was the greatest of all prophets and messengers. This was symbolically shown on the Night of Isrā wa al-Mi'rāj, when the Prophet ﷺ led the prayer of all previous prophets and messengers in Jerusalem.

6.2. Prophet Muhammad's superiority over other messengers.

The Prophet ﷺ himself expressed how Allāh granted him unique features not given to previous prophets and messengers. In a Hadīth recorded by Imām Muslim, he said he had distinction over other prophets through six things:

1. ***Jāmi Kalām.*** This refers to the ability to eloquently express a comprehensive meaning with few words. For example, the Prophet ﷺ explained the whole concept of intention in Islām using three words, انما الاعمال بالنيات.

2. **Assisted with *Ru'b.*** This means that even if the Prophet ﷺ was a month off in distance, his enemies would tremble in fear and awe of him.

3. **War spoils.** Previous Ummahs were not permitted to claim the spoils of war.

4. **Clean earth.** Followers of the Prophet ﷺ are permitted to read Salāh anywhere on earth and are permitted to perform *Tayammum* from it.

5. **Universality.** Previous prophets were sent for certain people. Our Prophet ﷺ was sent for all of mankind until the Day of Judgement.

6. **Finality.** The Prophet ﷺ is the seal of all prophets and messengers.

These six points are not the only means by which our Prophet ﷺ holds superiority over other prophets and messengers. Other key attributes and distinctions include:

- He is the only prophet to have his name on the *Arsh* (Throne).
- He is the only prophet to have been given an eternal miracle, in the form of the Qur'ān.
- He is the only prophet to have been sent to both men and jinns.

Suffice to say, Imām Jalāl al-Dīn Suyūtī (d. 911/1505) has written a detailed, two-volumed book called *al-Khasā'is al-Nabawiyya al-Kubrā*, listing his countless, unique features.[123]

6.3. Is the Prophet 'just a man like us'?

In several places in the Qur'ān, Allāh affirms that the Prophet ﷺ is a *Bashar* (human), just like all previous prophets and messengers (18:110). The reason for this is two-fold:

a. So they can be a role model for their subjects (4: 64). They can only be a successful model to follow if they share some resemblance with those required to follow them.

If Allāh were to send an angel instead of a man, then the followers would have legitimate reasons not to follow his example. They would claim that angels are made from divine light and are immune from sins, and therefore using them as a role model is impossible. The Qur'ān touches

123 *Al-Khasā'is al-Nabawiyya al-Kubrā*. Jalāl al-Dīn al-Suyūtī.

upon this when it states:

> 'And they say: 'Why has not an angel been sent down to him?'... And had We appointed him an angel, We indeed would have made him a man, and We certainly would have caused them confusion in a matter which they were already confused.' (6: 8-9)

Hence, Allāh ensured that all prophets and messengers were men so the disbelievers would have no reason not to follow them.

b. So people do not see him as a deity. Allāh affirmed that the Prophet ﷺ was a human being to prevent followers from perceiving him as God or the Son of God, like the Christians did. Jesus (peace be upon him) preached the oneness of Allāh and that he was the messenger of Allāh, but his followers distorted his message and invented the concept of trinity. Hence, it was imperative to clearly highlight that Muhammad ﷺ was a human being and not a deity.

In short, all prophets and messengers had to be human in order to preserve and protect the task of propagating Islām successfully.

But there is a very clear difference between when:

i. The Prophet ﷺ *himself* asserts that he is a human, like 'I am a man like you' (18: 110).

ii. When the followers call their prophets a human (*Bashar*). The reason is that when previous communities wanted to insult and degrade their prophets, they would call them humans. For example, Nūh's people said to him:

> 'We do not see you except a man (*Bashar*) like us.' (11:27)

Sālih's people said to him:

'You are but a human being (*Bashar*) like us.' (26: 154)

Sho'aib's people insulted him by saying:

'You are but a human (*Bashar*) like us and verily we think you are one of the liars.' (26: 186)

In Sūrah Yāsīn, Allāh tells how the people of the village rejected their messengers and ridiculed them:

'They said: You are only human being like ourselves, and the Most-Merciful has revealed nothing...' (36:15)[124]

In short, when the followers call their prophets human, it is a form of insult. When the prophet himself asserts he is human, then there is no harm and it is in fact a form of humility.

Yūnus (peace be upon him) was a prophet of Allāh and the chosen servant of His. The Qur'ān recalls one of his *Du'ā*s:

لا اله الا انت سبحانك اني كنت من الظالمين

'There is no God but you, Glorified are you; truly I have been from the wrong-doers.' (21:87)

Allāh does not love the wrong-doers (3:57), He does not guide such people (3: 86) and He curses them (7: 44). But Yūnus called himself a wrong-doer. The only correct interpretation for this is that when Yūnus calls himself a wrong-doer, then it is a sign of his humility, piety, modesty and humbleness. When someone else calls him a wrong-doer, then this is a sign of insult, ridicule and blasphemy. If a Muslim was to take the

124 Similar statements can be found in other places in the Qur'ān. See (i) 14:10 (ii) 15:33 (Iblīs stated that the reason why he would not prostrate to Adam because he was a *Bashar*), (iii) 21:3 (where the Arabs rejected the message of Muhammad by saying that 'is he but a human like you?') (iv) and 23:33.

exact same phrase and call Yūnus (peace be upon him) a *Zālim*, then this would render that person a non-Muslim.

The reason why this matter needs clarification is that some Muslims have taken this matter too far and as a result, risk insulting the Prophet ﷺ. They unfortunately assert that the Prophet is '*just* a man', or that the prophet is a 'man like us'. Such statements can earn the wrath of Allāh and as we have seen, these words are exactly what previous communities used to say before they were severely punished by Allāh.

To conclude, the Prophet ﷺ himself clarified that no one can claim to be like him. Imām al-Bukhārī reports in his *Sahīh* that the Prophet ﷺ once forbade his Companions from keeping continuous fasts.[125] One of the Companions enquired: 'O Messenger of Allāh! But you keep continuous fasts.' The Prophet replied:

> 'Who from amongst you is like me? When I go to sleep my Lord gives me food and drink.'[126]

The Prophet ﷺ is *Bashar* (human) but this is not a reason for us to view him as ordinary.

6.4. Muhammad; the Seal of all Prophets.

All Muslims unanimously agree that Muhammad ﷺ is the last prophet sent from Allāh. There will be no prophet or messenger after him.

This issue does not need further clarification and analysis, because the finality of the Prophet ﷺ is proven definitively from the Qur'ān and Sunna. Unfortunately, because people have appeared claiming to be a

---

125 In Arabic, this is called *al-Wisāl*. It means keeping a fast throughout the day and night for many days.
126 *Sahīh al-Bukhārī*. Book of Hudūd (punishments), Hadīth no. 6345.

prophet – like Mirza Ghulām Ahmad Qādiānī – it is important to clarify our position beyond doubt.

6.4.1. Who was Mirza Ghulām Ahmad and who are the Qādiānīs?

Mirza Ghulām Ahmad was born between 1835 and 1839 in the Indian village of Qādiān and died in 1908. He founded the Qādiānī sect, also known as the Mirzāīs or the Ahmadīs. His sect was founded on the belief that he was a prophet, God forbid.

His father served in the court of the Sikh ruler Ranjit Singh, who was later overthrown by the British. During his lifetime, the British colonised India and for people like Ghulām Ahmad, it became a reason to become totally dependant on them.

Some of the disbelieving comments made by him include:

- 'He who differentiates between Muhammad and myself and thinks of us as different has not understood or seen me' (*Khutba Ilhāmiyya*).
- 'Muhammad could not complete the mission of propagating Islām; I have fulfilled this mission' (*Hāshiya Tuhfa Ghoulariyya*).
- 'In the time of Muhammad, Islām was like the crescent of the moon on the first night. However, in my time Islām has become like the full moon on the fourteenth night' (*Khutba Ilhāmiyya*).
- 'The number of miracles performed by Muhammad was three thousand in number. But my miracles exceed ten thousand' (*Barāhīn Ahmadiyya*).
- 'My book *Barāhīn Ahmadiyya* is the word of Allāh' (*Izāla al-Awhām*).

- 'There are grammatical errors in the Qur'ān' (*Haqīqa al-Wahy*).
- He ascribed the verse 'And We have not sent you but a mercy for all the worlds' to himself. [127]
- Not only did Mirza Ghulām Ahmad commit *Kufr* by claiming to be a prophet, he directed insults to Īsā and Maryam (peace be upon them). He reportedly said that Jesus was in no way better than Kaushalya's son Ram. [128]

6.4.2. Evidence from the Holy Qur'ān that Muhammad is the last Messenger.

Allāh affirms in the Holy Qur'ān:

> 'Muhammad is not the father of any man among you, but he is the messenger of Allāh and the Seal (*Khātam*) of the Prophets. And Allāh is aware of everything.' (33:40) [129]

Elsewhere, Allāh says:

> 'Today I have perfected your *Dīn* for you and have completed my blessings upon you and have chosen Islām as a *Dīn* for you.' (5:3)

If Allāh has 'completed' the religion, what purpose is served by sending another prophet or messenger after Muhammad ﷺ?

---

127 All quotes cited in *La Nabiyya Ba'dī*. p. 46. Sahibzāda Sayyid Muhammad Amīn Alī Shāh.
128 pp. 218-9. *Sirat Ahl as-Sunnah*.
129 Arab linguists are unanimous in the meaning of the word *Khātam*. Imām Jawharī states that it means 'to affix, seal or close something'. Ibn Manzūr states in *Lisān al-Arab* that it means 'final'. Every Mufassir (commentator of the Qur'ān) has translated *Khātam* to mean 'final', including Ibn Jarīr al-Tabarī, Imām Fakruddīn Razī, Imām Jalāl al-Dīn Suyūtī, Allāma Ibn Kathīr and Allāma Alūsī. The commentators have also agreed that anyone who denies the finality of the Prophet (peace and blessings of Allāh be upon him) is not a Muslim.

6.4.3. Evidence from the Ahādīth.

There are countless Ahādīth in which the Prophet ﷺ asserts that he is the final Prophet. Imām al-Bukhārī narrates a Hadīth from Abū Huraira ؓ in which he reports that the Prophet ﷺ said:

> 'My position in relation to the prophets who came before me can be explained in the following example. A man erected a building and adorned his edifice with great beauty, but he left an empty niche, in the corner where just one brick was missing. People looked around the building and marvelled at its beauty, but wondered why a brick was missing from that niche. I am like that one missing brick and I am the last in line of the prophets.'[130]

Imām Tirmidhī (d. 279/892) has recorded a Hadīth in which the Prophet ﷺ said:

> 'The chain of messengers and prophets has come to an end. There shall be neither messenger nor prophet after me.'[131]

There are too many Ahādīth to mention here. In the nine most authentic books of Ahādīth, (*Sahīh al-Bukhārī, Sahīh Muslim, Sunan Tirmidhī, Sunan Ibn Māja, Sunan Nasā'ī, Sunan Abū Dāwūd, Musnad Ahmad, Muwatta Mālik, Sunan Dārmī*) there are over eighty Ahādīth which all explicitly mention that Muhammad ﷺ is the last Messenger.

---

130 *Sahīh al-Bukhārī*, Book of Virtues, Hadīth Number 3271. Imām Muslim and Imām Ahmad ibn Hanbal have also narrated this same Hadīth.

131 *Sunan al-Tirmidhī*, Kitāb al- Ru'ya (Dreams), Hadīth Number 2198. Imām Bukhārī, Imām Muslim, Imām Ibn Māja and Imām Ahmad ibn Hanbal have also narrated this same Hadīth.

6.4.4. Evidence from Common sense.

- Each prophet preached and delivered the guidance of Islām in a perfect manner but after his passing away, the people modified and altered the scriptures in line with their own desires and false beliefs. This led to the need for another prophet to once again restore and reiterate the true message of Islām. However, with the revelation of the Qur'ān, it was announced that there was no possibility of any modification or change in the text. Its each and every word was and will be protected until the Day of Judgement. Thus if the Qur'ān is to remain unaltered there is no need for another Prophet.

- In Islām, the concept of prophet-hood plays a crucial and fundamental role. A person's Īmān depends upon his views towards prophet-hood. He who believes in each and every prophet is considered a Muslim, and similarly, he who denies any of the prophets is a Kāfir. If we assume for one moment that there would be a prophet after Muhammad ﷺ, Allāh would have made it clear to all Muslims. He would have mentioned it clearly in the Qur'ān that there would be a Prophet after Muhammad ﷺ and there would be some indication in Ahādīth too. So if we are to believe the Qādiānī claim, why is there no mention of him in either the Qur'ān or Sunna? There is not even a weak Hadīth that supports the Qādiānīs. Instead, we find countless Ahadīth which all falsify the claim of Mirza Qādiānī and any other impostor. Both the Qur'ān and Sunnah are clear in explaining the finality of the Prophet ﷺ.

- A brief look at the life of Mirza Ghulām Ahmad shows that there are blatant contradictions and discrepancies in his claims. In 1882, he declared himself to be a *Mujaddid* (reviver of faith). Then in 1889, he claimed he was Mahdī, as well as the second coming of Jesus. Finally, he claimed in 1901 that he was a Prophet. Then after his death, the Ahmadīs in Lahore denied that Mirza Ghulām Ahmad had ever claimed prophet-hood, and that he was a Muslim saint and not a Prophet. How can Qādiānīs preach their message to others, when they themselves are unclear and confused about their own shallow beliefs?

- To those who show love, respect and adoration for the Prophet ﷺ, any such claim is baseless and futile. Allāh granted the Prophet ﷺ the most lofty of status, in both this world and the hereafter. His name adorns the heavens, the angels continually send blessings upon him, and the believers send salutations upon him. The Prophet ﷺ is the *magnum opus* of Allāh's creation. It seems illogical that a vile impostor like Mirza Qādiānī would eclipse a radiant character such as our Prophet ﷺ.

6.4.5. Conclusion.

The Prophet ﷺ himself – through his God-given knowledge – told us that there would unfortunately be false impostors. Imām al-Bukhārī reports from Abū Huraira:

> '...The Day of Judgement will not happen until lying *Dajjāl*s appear, close to thirty in number.' [132]

But this aside, it seems that Mirza Ghulām Ahmad was simply an opportunist and a product of his time. He lived at a time when Wahhābism and similar heretical beliefs were gaining popularity in India. He was a contemporary of Rashīd Ahmad Gangūhī (1829-1905), Ashraf Alī Thānwī (1863-1943), Moulāna Muhammad Ilyās, Qāsim Nanotwī (1832-1880), to mention a few names. All had in some form or another insulted and degraded the true status of prophet-hood. Qāsim Nanotwī, for example, explicitly wrote in his book *Tahzīr al-Nās* that if another prophet appears after Muhammad ﷺ, then it does not change

132 *Sahīh al-Bukhārī*. Book of superiorities, Hadīth no. 3340.

the fact that he is the seal of all prophets.[133] Ashraf Alī Thānwī said that 'there are certain attributes which are common between me and the Holy Prophet.'[134] He also said that 'the kind of knowledge of the unseen given by Almighty Allāh to the Holy Prophet has also been given to animals, lunatics and children.'[135]

Given this climate, Mirza Ghulām Ahmad thought that if the rank of prophet-hood was being projected as so low and ordinary, he too could claim to be one. Because the Wahhābīs and Deobandīs had propagated the Prophet ﷺ as being a mere mortal, he saw no reason why he too could not attain such a rank. In short, Muslims at the time began to belittle the status of the Prophet ﷺ to such an extent that an ignorant man like Mirza Ghulām Ahmad could claim to be a prophet.

The best means to preserve the finality of the Prophet ﷺ is to preserve his God-given high rank. This is the precise reason why no false impostors appeared in the middle ages of Islām; because this was the period when the scholars held the Prophet ﷺ in the highest regard. No one dared to question the finality of the Prophet ﷺ during the times of the likes of Imām Ghazālī (1058-1111), Qādi Iyādh (1147-1148), Imām Nawawī (1234-1278), Ibn Hajar al-Asqalānī (1372-1448), Imām Jalāl al-Dīn Suyūtī (1445-1505) Imām Sakhāwī (1428-1497) and Imām Qastalānī (1448-1517). Had Mirza Ghulām Ahmad lived during the period of any of these scholars, he would have been punished severely. Instead, because he lived in a climate where blasphemy towards the Prophet ﷺ was fashionable, his views were accepted by some Muslims.

---

133 Cited in *al-Aqīda al-Hasana (al-Mar'ūf bi) Aqā'id al-Islām* (p.96). Hazrat Shāh Walī Allāh Muhaddith Delhvī.

134 Cited in *Sirat Ahl as-Sunnah* (p.313). The original quote is from *Ifaazat al-Yaumiyya*, Part VII, p. 464.

135 *Hifz al-Iman*. p. 7. Cited in *Sirat Ahl as-Sunnah*. p. 320.

Chapter Seven

Belief in the Last Day

7. 1. Introduction.

It is obligatory for Muslims to believe in the Last Day; when Allāh Almighty will take the accounts of all humans and designate each person a place in heaven or hell. In the Qur'ān and Ahādīth, we are told of the different names of this day:

- ***al-Yaum al-Ākhir***. Because it is the last day. Thereafter there will be no real concept of time because people will live forever in either heaven or hell. Abū Sa'īd al-Khudrī ﷺ reports that the Prophet ﷺ said:

  > 'Death will be brought in the form of a ram that is more white than black on the Day of Judgement, and it will be placed in between Paradise and Hell. It will be said: 'O people of Paradise! Do you know what this is?' They will extend their necks to get a better view and will reply: 'Yes, this is death.' It will then be said: 'O people of Hell! Do you know what this is?' They will extend their necks to get a better view and will reply: 'Yes, this is death.' The ram will then be ordered to be slaughtered. It will then be said: 'O people of Paradise! Eternity, and no more death.

O people of Hell! Eternity, and no more death.'[136]

- ***Yaum al-Qiyāma*** (75:1). This means the Day of Standing, because everyone will arise from their graves for the questioning.

- ***Yaum al-Hisāb*** (14:41). This translates as the Day of Account.

- ***Yaum al-Hashr*** (59:2). This means the Day of Gathering.

In his *Ihyā Ulūm al-Dīn*, Imām Ghazālī (d. 505/1111) mentions over one-hundred names for this day.[137]

7.2. Logical proofs for the occurrence of the Day of Judgement.

We often see oppressive and tyrannical people who terrorise others, but then leave this world before receiving their due punishment. Conversely, there are countless people who are on the receiving end of oppression, but they are not rightly rewarded for their pains. If there was no hereafter, then the tyrant would be left unpunished and the oppressed would be left unrewarded. Such a situation is contrary to the wisdom of Allāh. Therefore it is imperative that another world exists where the tyrant will be duly punished and the oppressed will be duly rewarded.

In order to implement the notion of punishment and reward, the world we live in must cease. This is because punishment and reward can only be given once everyone's actions terminate. Until the actions of people and this world do not end, this system cannot take place.

---

136 *Sahīh Muslim*, Book of Paradise and the description of its blessings and inhabitants, Hadīth no. 5087.

137 p. 206, vol. V. *Ihyā Ulūm al-Dīn*. Abū Hāmid Muhammad ibn Muhammad al-Ghazālī (d. 505/1111). Abdul Hakim Murad has translated the entire chapter on the remembrance of death and the afterlife from *Ihyā* (*The Remembrance of Death and the Afterlife. Kitāb Dhikr al-Mawt wa mā ba'duhū*. T.J. Winter. Islamic Texts Society. 2006).

For example, Qābil[138] initiated the sin of murder, and he will receive the punishment of everyone who commits murder thereafter. So until murder does not end, the process of writing his bad acts cannot be finished. When a person builds a mosque, then he is rewarded for every person who performs worship in that mosque. When a person establishes a place of idol-worship, then his account cannot be concluded until everyone has utilised the place.

For this reason, so long as this world remains and the people in it, the accounts of people cannot be comprehensively concluded, something which needs to be done before punishment and reward. This is why the Day of Judgement exists. In short, the wisdom of Allāh stipulates that a system of punishment and reward should be established, and to implement this requires the Day of Judgement.[139]

7.3. The signs of the Last Day.

Allāh and His Messenger ﷺ have told us several signs before the Last Day. These are divided into two types;

a. *Sughra* (minor signs).

b. *Kubra* (major signs).[140]

It seems that the minor signs are general descriptions that are more open to interpretation, regarding what will happen nearer the Day of Judgement. The major signs are definitive events that will occur.

---

138 Cain, the son of Ādam (peace be upon him).

139 p. 98. *A Commentary of Sūrah Fātiha based on Tibyān al-Qur'ān*. Allāma Ghulām Rasūl Sa'īdī. Translated by Ather Hussain al-Azhari.

140 p. 382. *al-Sharh al-Qawīm fī Hall Alfāz al-Sirāt al-Mustaqīm*. Abd Allāh al-Hararī.

7.3.1. Some of the minor signs include:

i. A slave girl will give birth to her mistress.[141]

ii. Bare-footed, naked, poor, sheep-shepherds will compete with one another in erecting tall buildings.[142]

iii. An increase in earthquakes.

iv. An increase in illnesses that were not known to previous people.

v. People will appear claiming to be prophets.

vi. An increase in ignorance.

vii. An increase in murder and oppression.[143]

viii. The swift passing of time. Nearer to the Day of Judgement, time will pass very quickly so that a year will feel like a month. [144]

7.3.2. The major signs are:

i. The appearance of Mahdī. His name is Muhammad ibn Abd Allāh who will be from the descendants of Prophet Muhammad ﷺ.

ii. The appearance of Dajjāl. He will travel the earth causing havoc. However, he will be prohibited from entering Makka and Madina. Those who believe in him will experience unprecedented prosperity and wealth, and the believers who reject him will suffer from poverty.

---

141 *Sahīh Muslim*. Book of Faith, Hadīth no. 9.
142 Ibid.
143 pp. 382-3. *al-Sharh al-Qawīm fī Hall Alfāz al-Sirāt al-Mustaqīm*. Abd Allāh al-Hararī.
144 p. 53. *Islām: The Basic Articles of Faith, according to the Beliefs of the Ahl Sunna wa al-Jama'a; A Modern English Translation of Bahar-e-Shariat*. Part One. Over twenty minor signs are mentioned in this book (pp. 51-54).

He will trick people by his imagery of a garden and a fire. He will project the garden as heaven and the fire as hell, though in reality, the opposite will be true. The Muslims will not be deceived by him as they will be able to read the letters K-F-R on his forehead.[145]

iii. The descending of Prophet Īsā (peace be upon him). However, it is important to note that he will not appear in the capacity of a prophet, but as a follower of our Prophet ﷺ and he will rule with his Sharī'ah. He will kill the Dajjāl, smash the crucifix and outlaw swine. He will reside on earth for forty years and will then die. He will be buried in the Prophet's mosque in Madina Sharif.

iv. The appearance of Yājūj and Mājūj (Gog and Magog). These are two beastly tribes that will appear in the Far East. The Muslims will be saved from their terror by taking refuge on Mount Tūr.[146]

v. The rising of the sun from the west. When this happens, the door of repentance will be closed.

vi. The appearance of the beast of the earth (*Dābba al-Ard*).

vii. The smoke that will last on the earth for forty days.

viii. The sinking in the east, west and the Arab Peninsula.[147] This has been referred to as the *Khasaf.* A disastrous catastrophe will occur in which people will be swallowed by the earth.[148]

ix. The raising of the Qur'ān from the chests and from the books. When

---

145 pp. 55-56. *Islām: The Basic Articles of Faith, according to the Beliefs of the Ahl Sunna wa al-Jama'a; A Modern English Translation of Bahar-e-Shariat.* Part One.

146 p. 58. Ibid.

147 pp. 94-95. *Sharh al-Risāla al-Nāfi'a wa al-Hujaj al-Qāti'a.* Sheikh Muhammad Abd al-Latīf Sālih al-Farfūr (d. 1407/1986).

148 p. 51. *Islām: The Basic Articles of Faith, according to the Beliefs of the Ahl Sunna wa al-Jama'a; A Modern English Translation of Bahar-e-Shariat.* Part One.

this occurs, Khidr (peace be upon him) will die.[149]

x. A fire that will emit from Yemen.[150]

7.4. The Length of the Last Day.

In the Qur'ān, Allāh states the length of the Day of Judgement:

> 'The angels and the *Rūh* (Jibrā'īl) ascend to Him on a Day the measure whereof is fifty thousand years.' (70: 4)

Imām Abū Ya'la reports:

> 'Abū Sa'īd al-Khudrī ﷺ narrates that it was said to the Prophet ﷺ: 'O Messenger of Allāh! The Qur'ān mentions that the Day of Judgement will be the equivalent of fifty thousand years. How long is this day!' The Prophet ﷺ said:
>
> 'I swear by the Being whose hands control the soul of mine! The believer will be relieved on this day, to the extent it will feel as long as it takes to read the compulsory prayers of *Zuhr* in the previous life.'[151]

7.5. Our belief regarding the Gathering (*Hashr*).

It is *Wājib* (compulsory) that we believe in the Gathering; that all humans and jinns will be gathered for questioning.[152] The first person for whom the ground will open up for will be our beloved Prophet ﷺ whilst he is

149 p. 390. *al-Sharh al-Qawīm fī Hall Alfāz al-Sirāt al-Mustaqīm*. Abd Allāh al-Hararī.
150 *Sahīh Muslim*, Book of Calamities and the conditions of the Hour, Hadith no. 5162.
151 *Musnad Abū Ya'la*; cited in *A Commentary of Sūrah Fātiha based on Tibyān al-Qur'ān*. Allāma Ghulām Rasūl Sa'īdī. Translated by Ather Hussain al-Azhari (p. 96).
152 People shall be driven barefoot and naked to the place of Gathering, which will be white and perfectly smooth (p. 201, vol. V. *Ihyā Ulūm al-Dīn*, Imām al-Ghazālī).

alive in his grave. Each and every person will be full of immeasurable fright and anxiety. The sun will be above the heads of everyone which will lead to everyone drowning in sweat.[153] Seven types of people will be spared from the intensity of the heat and will take comfort in the *Shade of Allāh,* as explained by the Prophet ﷺ:

1. A just Imām.
2. A young Muslim who began to worship Allāh in his youth.
3. A man whose heart is attached to the mosque.
4. Two men who love each other for the sake of Allāh.
5. A man who remembers Allāh so much that he cries.
6. A man who is called by a women who possesses beauty or status but he refuses and says: 'I fear Allāh.'
7. And a man who gives *Sadaqa* secretly to such an extent that his left hand does not know what his right hand has given.[154]

7.6. The Accounting (*Hisāb*).

Allāh will call upon each person to justify his actions on the Day of Judgement. The Qur'ān states:

> 'Every soul will taste death. And you will be paid on the Day of Resurrection only that which you have fairly earned.' (3:185)

> 'And We suffice as reckoners.' (21:47)

---

153 pp. 202-3. vol. V. *Ihya Ulūm al-Dīn*, Imām al-Ghazalī.
154 *Sahīh al-Bukhārī.* Book of Raqā'iq. Hadīth no. 5998.

Allāh has made ten witnesses that will witness against mankind on the Day of Judgement. They are:

i. The tongues.

ii. The hands.

iii. The feet.

iv. The ears.

v. The eyes.

vi. The skin.

vii. The earth.

viii. The night.

ix. The day.

x. The angels appointed to each individual.[155]

The Qur'ān says:

> 'And they will say to their skins: 'Why do you testify against us?' They will say: 'Allāh has given us speech, He Who gives speech to all things, and Who created you at the first time, and to Whom you are returned. And you have not been hiding against yourselves, lest your ears and your eyes, and your skins testify against you, but you thought that Allāh knew not much of what you did.' (41: 21-22)

155 p. 99. *Sharh al-Risāla al-Nāfi'a wa al-Hujaj al-Qāti'a*. Sheikh Muhammad Abd al-Latīf Sālih al-Farfūr (d. 1407/1986).

> 'On the day when their tongues and their hands and their feet testify against them as to what they used to do.' (24:24)

However, when a Muslim repents sincerely to Allāh, then Allāh ensures there is no evidence against him on the Day of Judgement. Anas ﷺ reports that the Prophet ﷺ said:

> 'When a servant repents from his sins, then Allāh makes the angels forget about his sins, and He makes his body parts and anyone else (who knew) forget about the sins. This is to the extent that the servant meets Allāh on the Day of Judgement in the state that there is no evidence of sin against him.'[156]

7.7. The Scales.

Allāh says in the Qur'an:

> 'And the weighing on that day is true. So as for those whose scale of good deeds will be heavy, they will be the successful ones. And as for those whose scale will be light, they are those who will lose their own selves because they used to deny Our signs.' (7: 8-9)

The good and bad actions of every person will be written down on paper and this will be placed on the Scale, which will be governed by Jibrā'īl and Mikā'īl. Those fortunate people who have more good deeds than bad will find that the Scale weigh in their favour and thus will be saved from punishment. In a famous Hadīth recorded by Imām Muslim, the Prophet ﷺ said that reading *al-Hamdu Lillāh* abundantly is one way a person can weigh the Scales in his favour.[157]

---

156 p. 17. *Al-Muntakhabāt al-Imdādiyya*. M.I.H. Pirzada.
157 *Sahīh Muslim*, Book of Cleanliness, Hadīth no. 328.

7.8. The Bridge.

The *Sirāt* is a bridge that is situated above the fire of hell. From the Ahādīth, we are informed that this Bridge is as thin as a hair and as sharp as a sword. Everyone will be required to cross it, but as a reflection of their faith, they will do so at different speeds and ease. Some will shoot across it like a bolt of lightning whereas others will not be able to cross it.[158]

7.9. The Fountain *(Hawdh).*

After crossing the Bridge, the Prophet ﷺ will await for his followers at a pool called the *Hawdh*. In size, its length and width is a month's travel. The drinking vessels will be more in number than the stars in the sky. The drink will be whiter than milk, sweeter than honey and more fragranced than musk perfume. The Prophet ﷺ said that a person will never feel thirsty ever again after drinking from the *Hawdh.*[159]

7.10. The Intercession (*Shafā'a*).

Shafā'a means to ask someone for good on behalf of a third party.[160] The Qur'ān informs us that intercession will occur on the Day of Judgement, but only with Allāh's permission.[161] Prophet Muhammad ﷺ will perform intercession for the Muslim sinners and this plea will be accepted by Allāh.[162] His intercession will precede all other intercessions. This *Shafā'a*

---

158 p. 395. *al-Sharh al-Qawīm fī Hall Alfāz al-Sirāt al-Mustaqīm*. Abd Allāh al-Hararī.

159 p. 396. Ibid.

160 p. 405. Ibid.

161 In Ayat al-Kursī, Allāh states: 'Who is he that can intercede with Allāh except with His permission? (2: 255). There are several verses that prove that *Shafā'a* will certainly occur on the Day of Judgement (See 74:48, 7: 53). Verses that deny the existence of intercession on this Day refers to the disbelievers (see 26: 100); only the Muslims will be the successful recipients.

162 There are countless Ahādīth which conclusively prove that the Prophet (peace and blessings of Allāh be upon him) will perform intercession for the Muslim sinners on

will take on many forms:

7. 10.1. The Great Intercession.[163]

This great intercession will be on the Day of Judgement. People will throw themselves at the feet of prophets and messengers to intercede for them to their Lord.

Abū Huraira ﷺ narrates that: 'Some cooked meat was brought to Allāh's Messenger ﷺ and the meat of the forearm was presented to him as he used to like it. He ate a morsel of it and said:

> 'I will be the chief of all people on the Day of Judgement. Do you know the reason for it? Allāh will gather all the human beings of early generations as well as later generations on one plain so that the announcer will be able to make them all hear his voice and the watcher will be able to see them all. The sun will come so close to the people that they will suffer distress and trouble, as they will not be able to bear or stand. Then the people will say: 'Don't you see what state you have reached? Won't you look for someone who can intercede for you with your Lord?' Some people will say to some others: 'Go to Ādam (peace be upon him)'. So they will go to Ādam (peace be upon him) and say to him: 'You are the father of mankind, Allāh created you with his own hand, and breathed into you of his spirit (meaning the spirit which he created for you). And He also ordered the angels

the Day of Judgement. Anas ibn Mālik (may Allāh be pleased with him) reports that the Prophet (peace and blessings of Allāh be upon him) said: 'I am the first of the people to perform *Shafā'a* in paradise...' (*Sahīh Muslim*). Zaid ibn Arqam (may Allāh be pleased with him) reports from the Prophet (peace and blessings of Allāh be upon him) said: 'My intercession on the Day of Judgement is truthful. So he who does not believe in it has no right to it.' Cited in *Al-Radd alā Mustafā Mahmūd fī Inkār al-Shafā'a*. A. Muhdi ibn A. Qadir ibn A. Hadi. p. 34.

163 This is also referred to as the *Maqām Mahmūd* in the Holy Qur'ān and Ahādīth.

to prostrate before you, so please intercede for us with your Lord. Don't you see what state we are in? Don't you see what condition we have reached?' Ādam (peace be upon him) will say: 'Today my Lord has become angry as he has never become before, nor will ever become thereafter. He forbade me to eat the fruit of the tree but I disobeyed him. Myself! Myself! Myself! Go to someone else.' So they will go to Nūh (peace be upon him) and say to him: 'O Nūh (peace be upon him)! You are the first of Allāh's messengers to the people of the earth, and Allāh has named you a thankful slave, please intercede for us with your Lord. Don't you see what state we are in?' Nūh (peace be upon him) will say: 'Today my Lord has become angry as he has never become before or will thereafter. In the world I had the right to make one definitely-accepted prayer (*Du'ā*) and I made it against my nation. Myself! Myself! Myself! Go to someone else, go to Ibrāhīm (peace be upon him).' So they will go to Ibrāhīm (peace be upon him) and say: 'O Ibrāhīm! You are Allāh's Apostle and *Khalīl* from amongst the people of the earth so please intercede for us with your Lord. Don't you see what state we are in?' He will say to them: 'Today my Lord has become angry like never before or thereafter...Myself! Myself! Myself! Go to someone else. Go to Mūsā (peace be upon him).' So the people will go to Mūsā (peace be upon him) and will say: 'O Mūsā! You are Allāh's Apostle and he gave you superiority above the others with His message and with His direct talk to you. So please intercede for us, don't you see what state we are in?' Mūsā (peace be upon him) will say: 'My Lord today has become angry like never before or thereafter. I killed a person who I was not sanctioned to kill. Myself! Myself! Myself! Go to someone else, go to Īsā (peace be upon him).' So the people will go to Isā (peace be upon him) and will say: 'O Īsā (peace be upon him)! You are Allāh's Apostle and His word that he sent to Maryam, and a superior soul created by him, and you talked to the people whilst still in the cradle. So please intercede for us to your Lord, don't you see what state we are in?' Īsā (peace be upon him) will say: 'Today my Lord has become angry like never before or thereafter. Īsā (peace be upon him) will not mention any sin but will say 'Myself! Myself! Myself! Go to someone else; go to Muhammad (peace and blessings of Allāh be upon him).' So they will come to me and say: 'O Muhammad ﷺ! You are Allāh's Apostle and the last of the prophets and Allāh forgave your early and late sins. Please intercede for us with your Lord, don't you see what state we are in?' The Prophet ﷺ added: 'Then I will go beneath Allāh's throne and fall in prostration before my Lord. And then He will guide me to such praises and glorification's to Him, as He has never guided anybody else before me. Then it will be said: 'O Muhammad ﷺ! Raise your head. Ask and it will be granted. Intercede and your intercession will be accepted.' So I will raise my head and will say: 'My followers, O my Lord! My followers! O my Lord!' It will be said: 'O Muhammad ﷺ! Let those of your followers who have no accounts enter through such a gate of the gates of paradise as lies on the right, and they will share the other gates with the people.' The Prophet ﷺ further said: 'By him in whose hand is my soul, the distance between every two gate posts of paradise is like the distance between Makkah and Busra.'[164]

Abd al-Hādī, a professor at al-Azhar University, Cairo, writes after citing the above Hadīth:

'This Hadīth refutes numerous points that the deniers of *Shafā'a* purport. Firstly, *Shafā'a* is not *Shirk* with Allāh, nor is it independent from His order. Rather the Prophet ﷺ will prostrate

164 pp. 219-221 (vol. V). *Ihyā Ulūm al-Dīn*, Imām al-Ghazālī.

to Allāh and then praise Him with words which Allāh Himself inspires him to say. [Secondly], *Shafā'a* is not done according to the opinion of the Prophet ﷺ in that he personally chooses who exits the fire. Instead, Allāh sets the limits. [Thirdly], people should not depend on *Shafā'a* because it cannot save someone from entering the fire for a period of time. And whose skin can bear the fire of hell for even a moment? We ask forgiveness from Allāh.'[165]

Other forms of the Prophet's ﷺ intercession will be:

a. Intercession for those to enter paradise without the accounting.

b. Intercession to spare punishment from those who have had their accounting and are destined to Hell.

c. Intercession for the disobedient Muslims who believe in *Tawhīd*.

d. Intercession in the lightening of the punishment from the dwellers of the Fire, like Abū Tālib and others.[166]

Our Prophet ﷺ indicated many ways by which we can be subject to his intercession on the Day of Judgement;

a. By reading the Du'ā of Azān.[167]

اللهم رب هذه الدعوة التامة و الصلاة القائمة ات
محمد الوسيلة و الفضيلة و ابعثه مقاما محمودا

b. By visiting the blessed grave of the Prophet ﷺ. Imām Dāraqutnī

---

165 p. 32. *al-Radd alā Mustafā Mahmūd fī Inkār al-Shafā'a*. A. Muhdī ibn A. Qādir ibn A. Hādī.
166 p. 101. *Sharh al-Risāla al-Nāfi'a wa al-Hujaj al-Qāti'a*. Sheikh Muhammad Abd al-Latīf Sālih al-Farfūr (d. 1407/1986).
167 *Sahīh al-Bukhārī*, Book of Azān, Hadīth no. 579.

(d. 385/995) narrated in his *Sunan* from Ibn Umar ﷺ that the Prophet said:

> 'Whoever visits my grave, my intercession will be guaranteed for him.'[168]

c. By kissing the thumbs and wiping them on the eyes upon hearing Prophet Muhammad's ﷺ name. Al-Dehlmī reports in *al-Firdaus* that when Abū Bakr ﷺ heard the Prophet's name in Azān, he kissed his thumbs and wiped them on his eyes. The Prophet ﷺ said:

> 'Whoever does the same as my beloved has done (i.e. Abū Bakr), then my intercession has become permissible for him.'[169]

7.10.2. Other forms of intercession.

Other people and things will perform *Shafā'a* on the Day of Judgement. For example:

- Other prophets.
- The scholars.
- The martyrs.[170]
- The angels.[171]

---

168 Jibrīl Haddād wrote a comprehensive article outlining the sourcing of this Hadīth as well as other similar narrations extolling the virtue of visiting the Prophet's grave (www.livingislam.org).

169 pp. 440-1. *Al-Maqāsid al-Hasana*. Shams al-Dīn al-Sakhāwī (d. 902). Also cited in *Tashīh al-Aqā'id* (pp. 88-89), Muhammad Abd al-Hāmid Budāyūnī.

170 The Prophet ﷺ said: 'Three will perform intercession on the Day of Judgement; the prophets, then the scholars, then the martyrs.' (*Sunan Ibn Māja*, Book of *Zuhd*, Chapter, the mentioning of *Shafā'a*, Hadīth no. 4304).

171 *Sahīh Muslim*. Book of Faith, Hadīth no. 269.

- The Qur'ān.

- Fasting (*Sawm*).[172]

172 The Prophet (peace and blessings of Allāh be upon him) said: 'Fasting and the Qur'ān will perform intercession on the Day of Judgement for the servant. Fasting will say: 'O Lord! I stopped him from food and desires in the day, so please accept my intercession for him.' And the Qur'ān will say: 'I stopped him from sleeping at night, so please accept my intercession for him.' So their intercession will be accepted.' (*Musnad Ahmad*, Musnad of Abd Allāh ibn Amr al-Ās. Hadīth no. 6337).

Chapter Eight

Belief in Destiny *(Taqdīr)*

8. 1. Introduction.

There are two very important elements that we must keep in mind before looking at our belief in destiny.

a. The flawless knowledge of Allāh.

Firstly, we must wholly believe that Allāh's knowledge is perfect. He has the knowledge of what has happened and what will happen. Nothing occurs in the skies and heavens without His knowledge. The Qur'ān states:

> 'And with Him are the keys of the hidden (*Ghaib*), none knows them but He. And He knows whatever there is in the earth and in the sea. Not a leaf falls but He knows it.' (6:59)

b. This world is a test.

Secondly, we all accept that this world in which we are in is a test for humans. The Qur'ān states:

> 'Do you think that you will enter Paradise before Allāh tests

those of you who fought in His cause?' (3:142)

'You shall certainly be tried and tested in your wealth and in your personal selves...' (3: 186)

'Verily We have made that which is on earth as an adornment for it, in order that We may test them...' (18: 7)

It can only be a worthwhile test if we have some freedom to perform actions, whether good or bad. Otherwise there is no point in a system of reward and punishment.

Both of these points are very important in understanding the concept of destiny in Islām.

8.2. What is *Taqdīr*?

Before the creation of the universe, Allāh – with his eternal knowledge – wrote every good and bad deed. Whatever was to happen and whatever an individual, by his own choice and happiness, was to do, Allāh wrote it in the Preserved Tablet (*Lawh Mahfūz*). This is referred to as destiny or fate.[173] In Arabic, it is called *Qadr* or *Taqdīr*.[174]

However, it is not the case that whatever Allāh has written, that is what we have to do and that we are helpless and compelled to do exactly what He has written. Rather, whatever we are about to do by our own intention, choice and desire, that is what Allāh has written.[175]

---

173 p. 100. *Reflections: A Quest for Answers to Today's Questions.* M.I.H. Pirzada.

174 In a Hadīth recorded by Imām Tirmidhī, the Prophet (peace and blessings of Allāh be upon him) said: 'Indeed the first thing Allāh created was the pen. Allāh said to the pen: 'Write!' The pen replied: 'What shall I write?' Allāh said: 'Write down the *Qadr*; of everything that has happened and what will ever happen until the end of time' (Book of Fate, Hadīth no. 2081).

175 p. 100. *Reflections: A Quest for Answers to Today's Questions.* M.I.H. Pirzada.

8.3. The sensitivity surrounding *Taqdīr*.

Taqdīr is very difficult to understand and sometimes leads to many unanswered questions. The true secrets of this issue cannot be comprehended by most people. This is why Umar ﷺ strictly forbade any arguments on the topic of *Taqdīr* during his caliphate.[176]

Owing to its complexities, we are not required to have a detailed and comprehensive understanding of *Taqdīr*. Rather, like the Prophet ﷺ said, we simply need to 'believe in Qadr, the good and bad of it.'

This itself is a form of mercy from our Lord. In Islām, matters which are difficult to understand, like the soul for example, are exempt from our responsibilities.

8.4. The different sects on *Taqdīr*.

On the issue of *Taqdīr* in particular, there were two main sects in early Islām, both holding extremist views on the issue. The Ahl al-Sunna, however, occupies the middle ground.

8.4.1. Al-Jabariyya.

In short, they believed that man is compelled and constrained like a mere stone and has no free will of his own. Hence, whatever good or bad Allāh has written for a person, he is forced and obliged to do just that.

This belief is contrary to Islām since Allāh has granted every human free will and the choice to perform good or bad. If this freedom was not granted, there would have been no need to send prophets to show people

---

176 p.13. *Islām: The Basic Articles of Faith, according to the Beliefs of the Ahl Sunna wa al-Jama'a; A Modern English Translation of Bahar-e-Shariat.*

right from wrong. Rūmī gives an example to show the shallowness of this position:

> 'A person who belonged to the Jabariyya sect once passed by a garden. He felt hungry and so he entered the garden and began eating its grapes. The owner of the garden happened to arrive and caught this person eating his grapes. 'How dare you eat from my garden without permission?' He replied: 'Without the permission of Allāh, no leaf can come into existence. This is God's garden, I am God's servant and I am eating with God's permission and command. I have no choice. Go and ask Him as to why He is making me eat.' Upon this response, the owner tied up the person's feet and hands and began to beat him with a stick. 'You are being cruel and tyrannical!' he shouted. The owner responded: 'Just like you, I am also compelled and constrained. The sticks of God, with God's permission, are falling upon you!' After this episode, the person repented from his heretical beliefs.' [177]

After citing this story, Rūmī (d. 671/1273) concluded:

> 'O human being! If you throw a stone at a dog, the dog will not attack the stone but will attack you. The dog is aware that the stone is constrained and has no free will whereas you possess free will and can do as you please. O naïve human being! A dog can differentiate between you and a stone. If you cannot see the difference, then you are no better than a foolish dog!'[178]

One can see how this viewpoint leads to apathy and neglect in religion. Why should Zaid perform Salāh when Allāh has already written that He will not read Salāh? Why strive for a bright hereafter when Allāh has

---

177 p. 104. *Reflections: A Quest for Answers to Today's Questions.* M.I.H. Pirzada.
178 Ibid.

already written where we are destined for and we cannot reverse that?

8.4.2. Al-Qadariyya.

This refers to an early group of Muslims who showed extremist tendencies in their belief in *Taqdīr*. They believed that humans have independent power and autonomy, and that they are not dependent on divine help in their actions. This belief is contrary to Islām since only Allāh Almighty possesses complete authority and autonomy.

The first person to conceptualise *Taqdīr* in such a way was Ma'bad al-Juhanī. He used to sit in the gatherings of Hasan al-Basrī. Under the orders of Abd al-Malik Marwān, he was punished for his extremist views and was crucified in 80 A.H. [179]

In order to refute this position, there is a famous story with Ali ﷺ and a man who had Qadariyya beliefs:

> 'One day a person came to him and stated that a human is all-powerful and can do as he pleases. Ali ordered: 'Lift one of your legs up and stand on the other.' The person did as instructed. Then Ali said: 'Leave this leg raised and lift the second leg up.' The person replied: 'If I try that I will fall to the ground.' In response, Ali said: 'It is just this much free will which humans possess. If man was all-powerful, he would be able to raise both feet in the standing position.'[180]

---

179 pp. 17-18. *Sharh al-Risāla al-Nāfi'a wa al-Hujaj al-Qāti'a*. Sheikh Muhammad Abd al-Latīf Sālih al-Farfūr (d. 1407/1986).

180 p. 105. *Reflections: A Quest for Answers to Today's Questions*. M.I.H. Pirzada.

8.4.3. The Ahl al-Sunna.

The Ahl al-Sunna rejects the extreme views held by the Jabiriyyas and Qadariyyas and occupies the middle ground. Allāh Almighty has predestined every good thing and every bad thing in accordance with His eternal and perfect knowledge. He has ordained everything. This, however, does not imply that what we do is predestined to be done by us. On the contrary, it implies that Allāh predestines what we are to do.[181]

Concerning the future, Allāh has written the fate of every individual with His perfect knowledge, that x will perform such and such action at this time. *Taqdīr* has no compelling power in this. The decision belongs to the individual person and he himself is responsible for the resulting reward or punishment for his action. Allāh, through his perfect knowledge, has simply recorded it in advance.[182]

It is up to every individual whether he chooses to do good, for which he will be rewarded, or to do bad, for which he will be punished. There are certain things in which we are helpless and simply cannot change, like life and death, where a person is born, where he dies and physical appearance. But no individual will be questioned or held responsible for such things.[183]

8.5. Possible Objections.

a. In Sūrah Baqara, Allāh states:

> 'Indeed, the ones who have chosen disbelief in Islām will not believe (in Allāh), whether you warn them or not. Allāh has

---

181 p.10. *Islām: The Basic Articles of Faith, according to the Beliefs of the Ahl Sunna wa al-Jama'a; A Modern English Translation of Bahar-e-Shariat.*

182 p. 101. *Reflections: A Quest for Answers to Today's Questions.* M.I.H. Pirzada.

183 p. 105. Ibid..

sealed their hearts and ears. And there is a veil on their hearts. And they shall be subject to a great torment.' (2: 6-7)

This verse seemingly seems unfair. Since Allāh has already sealed their hearts and proclaimed them as disbelievers, it will not be possible for them to accept Islām.

Answer:

In answer to this, we can compare their situation to a patient whose doctor proclaims that his illness is incurable. Has the patient become incurable due to the doctor's declaration, or due to the illness now reaching its terminal stage? Clearly, the patient has already become incurable due to the extent of the illness and the doctor merely informed the patient of his critical state. In the same manner, these people had already decided that they are not going to accept Islām, due to their staunchness. Allāh merely informed us of their intentions and state.[184]

b. In the Holy Qur'ān, it seems there are verses contradicting one another regarding *Taqdīr*.

> 'And if some good reaches them, they say: 'This is from Allāh', but if some evil befalls them, they say: 'This is from you (O Muhammad!)' Say: All things are from Allāh...' (4: 78)

In the next verse, Allāh states:

> 'Whatever of good reaches you is from Allāh. But whatever evil befalls you is from yourself.' (4: 79)

The first verse suggests that any favour or mishap a person experiences is from Allāh. The second verse states that favours come from Allāh,

---

184 p. 102. Ibid.

whereas evil come from people themselves. This apparently seems like a contradiction.

Answer:

The first verse means that Allāh is the *Creator* of all actions, good and bad. The second verse refers to the *cause* of good and evil. This lies in human hands.

Also, Allāh does create both good and evil, though sometimes we choose not to mention evil out of respect.

Chapter Nine

Belief in Resurrection after death

9. 1. Introduction.

It is our belief as Muslims that each and every soul will experience death. The Qur'ān states:

> 'Every soul shall taste death.' (3:185)

Even the angel of death will take his own soul with the order of his Lord, and then there will be no one left alive on the face of the earth.[185]

It is incumbent to believe that whoever dies, does so with the reason of predestination. Allāh states:

> 'When their appointed time has come, then they cannot delay it an hour nor precede it an hour.' (10:49)

Even if a person dies from a disease or another reason, he does so at an appointed time. He cannot precede it or delay it.

---

185 p. 95. *Sharh al-Risāla al-Nāfi'a wa al-Hujaj al-Qāti'a*. Sheikh Muhammad Abd al-Latīf Sālih al-Farfūr (d. 1407/1986).

9.2. Resurrection after death.

As Muslims, we believe that Allāh Almighty has the power to revive the dead from the grave, on the Day of Judgement. This is referred to as *al-Ba'th ba'd al-Mawt.* To those who refute the possibility of this happening, the Qur'ān states:

> '[The disbeliever] says: 'Who will give life to these bones when they have rotted away and have become dust?' Say (O Muhammad): 'He will give life to them Who created them in the first place! And He is the All-Knower of all creations.' (36: 78-9)

Elsewhere, Allāh states:

> 'From [the earth] We created you, and into it We shall return you, and from it We shall bring you out once again.' (20:55)

9.3. What is death (*Mawt*)?

Because of the way language works, we tend to associate death with nothingness. Death is the opposite of life; when we are alive, we can see, hear and feel things. Therefore we tend to think that when a person is dead, he cannot do anything at all. Islām's position is different to this approach. Imām Qurtubī (d. 671/1272) defines *Mawt* when he writes:

> 'Death (*Mawt*) does not mean mere nothingness. Rather, it means the transferral from one state to another.'[186]

In other words, death only implies departure from this world. It does not mean total obliteration or non-existence after death.[187]

---

186 p. 91. Cited in *al-Isrā wa al-Mi'rāj*. Dr. Abd al-Halīm Mahmūd.
187 p 44. *Islām: The Basic Articles of Faith, according to the Beliefs of the Ahl Sunna wa al-Jama'a; A Modern English Translation of Bahar-e-Shariat*. Part One.

9.4. Those people whose bodies will not decay in the grave.

As a sign of acceptance and proximity to Allāh Almighty, there are certain people whose bodies do not perish in their graves. They are:

1. The prophets & messengers.
2. The martyrs.
3. The scholars who act upon their knowledge.
4. The callers to the prayers (*Muezzin*).
5. The memorisers of the Qur'ān who act upon what is revealed in it.[188]
6. The *Awliyā* (saints of Allāh).[189]

9.5. Our belief regarding the questioning in the grave.

It is compulsory that we believe in the questioning in the grave after death, for Muslims and non-Muslims.

When the burial has taken place and the deceased's family leaves the graveyard, the deceased hears their footsteps as they leave. Then two angels will appear after the burial, called *Munkar* and *Nakīr*. The soul will be made to return to the person and he will be brought back to life. They will ask him about his Lord, his religion and about the man who was sent amongst them (namely the Prophet ﷺ).

---

188 p. 96. *Sharh al-Risāla al-Nāfi'a wa al-Hujaj al-Qāti'a*. Sheikh Muhammad Abd al-Latīf Sālih al-Farfūr (d. 1407/1986).

189 p. 378. *al-Sharh al-Qawīm fī Hall Alfāz al-Sirāt al-Mustaqīm*. Abd Allāh al-Hararī.

The believer will say: 'My Lord is Allāh, my Religion is Islām and our beloved, our master Muhammad ﷺ was sent amongst us and indeed I believed in him.' Then it will be said to him: 'Look at your abode in paradise and now sleep peacefully pleased!' Then he will sleep in his grave until the Day of Gathering and a window will be opened from paradise. He will live in happiness and delight. The space of the grave will also be extended for the believer.

As for the non-Muslim, he will be asked the same as the Muslim but he will say: 'I don't know' to every question. As a result, he will be punished in his grave until the gathering and Allāh will send snakes and insects in his grave which will sting and bite him. Thereafter a window from the fire of hell will be opened and he will be punished like this until the Day of Gathering. The grave will become tight and restricted for him.[190] The Prophet ﷺ said:

> 'The graves are either gardens from the gardens of paradise or pits from the pits of hell.'[191]

9.5.1. The people who will not be questioned in their graves.

1. The prophets & messengers.
2. The martyrs.
3. The Muslims who are killed in oppression, namely, killed by another person without reason.
4. The Muslims who die in a plague.

---

190 p. 371. *al-Sharh al-Qawīm fī Hall Alfāz al-Sirāt al-Mustaqīm*. Abd Allāh al-Hararī.
191 *Sunan al-Tirmidhī*. Chapter: the Description of Qiyama. Hadīth no. 2384.

5. The truthful (*Siddiq*).
6. Muslim children.
7. The Muslims who die on a Friday or on Friday night.
8. The one who recites Sūrah Mulk every night.
9. The one who recites Sūrah Ikhlās at the time of his final illness.

As for the questioning of non-Muslim children and whether they enter heaven or hell, the scholars have differed over this. The correct opinion is that they are in the will of Allāh Almighty, and we leave their matter in His hands.[192]

9.6. *Barzakh* and the punishment/reward in this world.

Barzakh is the name given to the period between death and the resurrection. We sometimes talk about the *Ālam Barzakh* (world of Barzakh), when referring to this period.

According to his faith and actions in the previous life, a person will either enjoy the favours of Allāh during this period or he will be punished. Imām al-Bukhārī and Muslim report from Ibn Abbās ﵄ that:

> 'The Prophet ﷺ once passed by two graves and said: 'Both are being punished over trivial matters.[193] As for one of them, he never took care when urinating. As for the other, he used to tell-tale.' The Prophet then asked for a wet plant which he snapped

192 p. 98. *Sharh al-Risāla al-Nāfi'a wa al-Hujaj al-Qāti'a*. Sheikh Muhammad Abd al-Latīf Sālih al-Farfūr (d. 1407/1986).

193 In other words, people see them as trivial where in fact they are major sins.

in half. He placed them on the graves and said: 'Perhaps their punishment will be lightened until the plant withers.' [194]

On the other hand, the souls of the martyrs will reside in small birds that fly around the Throne of Allāh.[195]

In *Barzakh*, different souls are kept at different places according to their degree and status. Some souls will reside in the graves whilst others will live between the sky and earth. Other fortunate souls will reside in the gardens of paradise. The souls of the disbelievers will live in a place of punishment beneath the earth called *Sijjīn*.[196]

9.7. The sustained life of all Prophets in the grave.

From the Ahādīth and the opinions of the classical scholars, there is no doubt that all the prophets enjoy a sustained life after leaving this world.

a. Imām al-Nasā'ī (d. 303/915) narrates from Aws ibn Aws ﷺ that the Prophet ﷺ said:

> 'The best of your days is the day of Friday. On this day Ādam was created and on this day he died...so send salutations upon me as much as possible on this day. For verily your Salām is presented to me.' The Companions asked: 'And how will our salutations be presented to you when you pass away?' The Prophet ﷺ said: 'Verily Allāh has forbidden the earth to consume the bodies of

194 *Sahīh al-Bukhārī*. Book of Wudū (Ablution), Chapter: what has been mentioned about urinating. Hadīth no. 211. Imam al-Khattābī said: 'From this report we learn that it is *Mustahab* (preferred) to recite the Holy Qur'ān at the graves. If one can expect relief from the punishment with the *Tasbīh* (remembrance of God) of the plant, then certainly the recitation of the Qur'ān is greater in terms of expected-benefit and in terms of blessings (*Umda al-Qārī*: Vol. II, p. 118).

195 p. 378. *al-Sharh al-Qawīm fī Hall Alfāz al-Sirāt al-Mustaqīm*. Abd Allāh al-Hararī.

196 p 46. *Islām: The Basic Articles of Faith, according to the Beliefs of the Ahl Sunna wa al-Jama'a; A Modern English Translation of Bahar-e-Shariat*. Part One.

the prophets.' [197]

Imām al-Qushairī (d. 465/1072) adds that 'there is only purpose behind conveying Salām if the Prophet ﷺ is alive.'[198]

b. Anās ؓ reports that the Prophet ﷺ said:

> 'The prophets are alive, performing Salāh in their graves.'[199]

c. After the martyrdom of Imām Hussain ؓ, Yazīd led an assault against the people of Madina which resulted in Salāh being suspended from the Prophet's mosque. Sa'īd ibn Musayyab took shelter in the Prophet's resting place in the mosque and knew of the Salāh times only through the means of the Azān and Iqāma emitting from the Prophet's grave.[200]

d. Imām al-Qurtubī (d. 671/1272) supports the belief that prophets are alive when he writes:

> '[T]he martyrs after their death are alive, are given sustenance, are happy and give glad-tidings to others [as mentioned in the Qur'ān]. This [type of life] is of resemblance to people who are alive in this world. When it is established that martyrs are alive after death, then prophets are most certainly alive. And indeed it is proven conclusively that the earth does not consume the bodies of prophets, and that the Prophet ﷺ met the [previous] prophets on the Night of Isrā in Bayt al-Muqaddas and in the skies, and that he saw Mūsā (peace be upon him) performing Salāh in his grave and offered his salutations to the Ummah, to mention just a few sources of evidence. The 'death of prophets'

197 *Sunan al-Nasā'ī*. Hadīth no. 1357. Book of Juma; Chapter; Sending Salāh upon the Prophet excessively.
198 p. 88. *al-Isrā wa al-Mi'rāj*, Dr. Abd al-Halīm Mahmūd.
199 p. 369. *al-Sharh al-Qawīm fī Hall Alfāz al-Sirāt al-Mustaqīm*. Abd Allāh al-Hararī.
200 p. 32. *Tashīh al-Aqā'id*. Muhammad Abd al-Hāmid Budāyūnī.

is correct only in the sense that they are hidden from our sights. Otherwise, they are undoubtedly alive. Rather like the angels; for indeed they are present though no one from us can see them, except those who have been privileged by Allāh from his *Awliya*.'[201]

e. Imām Jalāl al-Dīn al-Suyūtī (d. 911/1505) writes:

> 'The Prophet ﷺ is alive with body and soul. He can go wherever he wants in the spaces of the earth and the [heavenly] kingdoms. Nothing has changed from his state before death and after. All of the prophets have been granted permission to leave their graves and move around the earthly and heavenly world. The sustained life of the Prophet ﷺ and indeed all of the prophets is proven definitively according to us, owing to the substantial evidence in support of this.'[202]

f. Imām Qastalānī (d. 923/1517) writes:

> 'There is no difference between the Prophet's life and death in looking over his Ummah, knowing their states, their intentions, their convictions and their inner feelings. This is all radiant to him without anything hidden.'[203]

g. Qādi Iyādh (d. 544/1149) writes:

> 'There is no doubt that the sustained life of the prophets (peace be upon them) is proven and known. And of course, our Prophet ﷺ is the best of all prophets.' [204]

---

201 p. 91. Cited in *al-Isrā wa al-Mi'rāj*, Dr. Abd al-Halīm Mahmūd.
202 p. 28. Cited in *Tashīh al-Aqā'id*. Muhammad Abd al-Hāmid Budāyūnī.
203 p. 28. Ibid.
204 p. 29. *Tashīh al-Aqā'id*. Muhammad Abd al-Hāmid Budāyūnī.

h. We find that Sheikh Ibn Taymiyya (d.728/1327) too agrees. It is mentioned in *Wafā al-Wafā*:

> 'Ibn Taymiyya mentioned in *Iqtidhā al-Sirāt al-Mustaqīm*, like it has been cited by Ibn Abd al-Hādī, that the martyrs, and in fact all believers, know and recognise the visitors and return the Salām when they come to visit and send greetings upon them. When this is the state of the [ordinary] believers, then how will it not be the case for the leader of all prophets ﷺ?' [205]

9.8. Do the dead benefit from the endeavours of the living? The issue of *Īsāl Sawāb*.

According to the majority opinion of the *Ahl al-Sunnah,* Muslims that have passed away can benefit from the prayers and actions of the living (*Īsāl Sawāb*). This is proven conclusively from the Holy Qur'ān, the sayings of the Beloved Prophet ﷺ and the consensus of the Ummah.

In general, the receiving of reward is achieved by one of two means.

i. The fruit of the deceased's actions in his own lifetime.

ii. The prayer (*Du'ā*) of Muslims for the deceased and the asking for forgiveness (*Istighfār*), as well as forms of charitable donations (*Sadaqa*) and worship (e.g. Hajj).

The people of innovation hold the view that a dead person cannot benefit at all, from a *Du'ā* or a good action.

---

205 p. 29. Ibid.

9.8.1. Proof of *Īsāl Sawāb* from the Holy Qur'ān.

Allāh Almighty says in the Qur'ān;

> 'And those who come after them say: 'Our Lord! Forgive us and our brothers who came before us into faith, and do not leave a sense of injury in our hearts against those, the believers. Our Lord! You are indeed most Kind and Merciful.' (59: 10)

Here, Allāh applauds those Muslims who prayed for their Muslim predecessors in the form of asking forgiveness for them. This proves that their asking for forgiveness does bring the deceased benefit and reward, since if it did not, Allāh would not have praised them.

9.8.2. Proof of *Īsāl Sawāb* from the Sunna.

There are countless Ahādīth which clearly indicate that *Īsāl Sawāb* is permissible.

a. The Prophet ﷺ would pray for the deceased Muslims. Imām Muslim records the *Du'ā*:

> اللهم اغفر له و ارحمه و عا فه و اعف عنه و أكرم نزله و و سع مدخله...
>
> 'O Allāh! Forgive him, and have mercy upon Him, and pardon him and show hospitality to him and make his grave spacious...'[206]

The Prophet ﷺ made a habit of praying for the deceased. Imam Muslim reports that the Mother of the Faithful, Ā'isha (may Allāh be pleased with her) said:

---

206 *Sahīh Muslim*. Book of Funeral Prayers, Chapter, the *Du'ā* for the deceased in Salāh.

'Whenever the Prophet stayed the night with me, he would go the Baqī (the graveyard in Madina Sharif) during the last part of the night and would say: 'Peace be upon you, the resting place for the believing ones! Your promised outcome will be seen tomorrow. We, if Allāh wills, shall soon join you. O Allāh! Forgive the people of Baqī al-Gharqad.'[207]

b. In a Hadīth recorded by both Imām Muslim and Bukhārī and narrated by Ā'isha (may Allāh be pleased with her) a person came to the Prophet ﷺ and said: 'My mother died suddenly and did not leave a bequest and I think if she had the opportunity she would have left some donations. Will she get a reward if I donate on her behalf? The Prophet ﷺ said: 'Yes.'[208]

Nor can it be said that the principle of transferring reward only applies to optional (*Nafl*) acts, such as charitable donations. We learn from Prophetic sayings that compulsory worship such as Hajj and fasting can be performed on behalf of a deceased too.

c. In *Sahīh al-Bukhārī*, Ibn Abbās ﷺ reports that a woman from Juhaiyna came to the Prophet ﷺ and said: 'My mother promised to perform Hajj, but did not get the chance to do so before she died. Can I perform Hajj on her behalf?'

The Prophet ﷺ replied: 'Yes, perform Hajj on her behalf. If she had an outstanding debt, would you not pay this off? Fulfill (the rights of) Allāh, for His promises are more important to fulfill.'[209]

---

207 *Sahīh Muslim*, Book of Funeral Prayers, Chapter: 'what is said upon entering the graveyard and praying for its inhabitants', Hadīth no. 1618. Al-Ghargad here is a description of Baqī and it means thorny bushes. The Prophet (peace and blessings of Allāh be upon him) described the graveyard of Madina as Baqī' al-Gharghad because of the large number of such bushes to be found there. See Imam Nawawi's commentary of *Sahīh Muslim* under this Hadīth.

208 *Sahīh al-Bukhārī*, Book of Funeral Prayers, Hadīth no. 1299.

209 *Sahīh al-Bukhārī*, Book: Adherence to the Book (of Allāh) and the Sunna, Hadīth 6671.

d. As for the reward of fasting for the deceased, both Imām Bukhārī and Muslim report that the Prophet ﷺ said:

> 'Whoever dies and has not fulfilled his (compulsory) fasts, then his representative should complete it on his behalf.' [210]

e. Jābir ؓ he reports that he read Eid al-Adhā Prayer with the Prophet ﷺ. After the Prayer, a ram was bought to the Prophet ﷺ which he sacrificed. As he did so he pronounced: 'In the name of Allāh; Allāh is the greatest. O Lord! This sacrifice is from myself and from whoever has not made a sacrifice from my Ummah.'[211]

In another narration from Imām Muslim, the Prophet ﷺ said: 'O Allāh! Please accept this from Muhammad, from the family of Muhammad and from the Ummah of Muhammad.' [212]

9.8.3. Proof of *Īsāl Sawāb* from *Ijmā* (Consensus) and from the scholars.

a. The scholars of Islām have unanimously agreed on the legitimacy of Funeral prayer (*Salāh al-Janāza*). In essence, this is but a supplication for the deceased. During the actual prayer, supplications are recited asking for the forgiveness of the deceased Muslim.

b. Imām Ahmad ibn Hanbal (d. 241/855) was asked about someone who performs good acts such as Salāh or *Sadaqa* and then dedicates some of the reward to his mother or father. He replied: 'I expect this to benefit' or he said: 'The deceased receives everything from the *Sadaqa* and its likes.' He also recommended to:

---

210 *Sahīh al-Bukhārī*. Book of Fasts. Chapter, He who dies without having fulfilled his fasts, Hadīth no. 1816.

211 *Sunan Tirmidhī*. Book of Sacrifices. Chapter, an Aqīqa with a goat, Hadīth no. 1441.

212 p. 125. *Tashīh al-Aqā'id*. Muhammad Abd al-Hāmid Budāyūnī.

'Recite Āyat al-Kursī three times, Sūrah Ikhlās and say *Allāhuma Inna Fadhlahu le Ahl al-Maqābir.*[213]

c. Ibn Taymiyya (d. 728/1327) said:

'As for righteous acts there is no conflict amongst the *Ahl Sunna wal Jamā'at* scholars that financial worships like charitable donations and the freeing of slaves do reach the deceased, just like Du'ā, Istighfār and Salāh al-Janāza and supplications at the grave benefit them too.

The difference of opinion is in physical worships such as fasting, Qur'ānic recitation and Salāh. The correct opinion is that all such worships benefit the deceased. It is proven in *Sahīh al-Bukhārī* and *Sahīh Muslim* that the Prophet ﷺ said: 'Whosoever dies and has not kept his [obligatory] fasts, then his guardian should fast on his behalf.' In a similar report, the Prophet ordered a woman to keep fasts on behalf of her deceased mother who had some delayed fasts incumbent on her.

In the *Musnad* of Ahmad, the Prophet ﷺ was reported to have said to Amr ibn al- Ās: 'Your father, if he had believed in monotheism (*Tawhīd*), and you then fasted for him, or had given *Sadaqa* on behalf of him, or had freed slaves on behalf of him, it (i.e. the reward) would have reached him.' This is the *Mazhab* of Imām Ahmad, Imām Abū Hanīfa and a large group of scholars from the Companions of Imām Mālik and Imām Shāfi'ī.'[214]

d. Allāma Taftazānī (d. 793/1390) summarises the debate on *Īsāl Sawāb*:

213 p. 37. *Islām Dīn al-Wastiyya wa al-I'tidāl* (Glossary for National Curriculum for Religious Teaching) Religious Endowment Department, Syria.
214 p. 366. *Kutub wa Rasā'il wa Fatāwa ibn Taymiyya fī al-Fiqh*. Vol. XXIV.

'And in *Du'ā* by the living for the dead and the giving of *Sadaqa* for them is a benefit...We have in support of our position authenticated Ahādīth regarding the prayer for the dead, especially the Salāh al-Janāza...If there had been no advantage for the dead in this prayer, there would be no point in performing it. The Prophet ﷺ said: 'No group of Muslims amounting to a hundred in number performs Salāh al-Janāza over the deceased, all of them interceding for him, without their intercession for him being welcomed.' Sa'd ibn Ubāda reported: 'O Messenger of Allāh! Umm Sa'd has died. What *Sadaqa* is best for her?' The Prophet ﷺ replied: 'Water.' So Sa'd dug a well and said: 'This is for Umm Sa'd.'...The Prophet ﷺ also said that if the learned and the learner pass by a village, Allāh will remove the torment from the cemetery of that village for forty days.' [215]

9.8.4. Objection.

The Qur'ān states:

'There is nothing for a man except what he strives for.' (53: 39)

This therefore suggests that when a person dies, only his own good deeds will be of benefit to him. The efforts of the living will not reach him.

Answer:

This verse does not contradict the majority position that *Īsāl Sawāb* is legitimate in Islām. The proof is in the famous saying of the Prophet:

'When a person dies, his actions cease except for three; continuous donations (*Sadaqa Jāriya*), a pious son who prays

215 pp. 171-172. *Sharh al-Aqā'id al-Nasfiyya*. Allāma Sa'd al-Din al-Taftazānī.

for him, or knowledge by which others benefit from him.'

All of these three things will benefit him in the afterlife because *during* his life, he took the necessary steps to ensure they would. Through his *own* effort, and during his life, he spent his money on charitable donations so that it would be of worth to him after dying. During his life, he nurtured his children and taught them the importance of praying for all Muslims, including the deceased. During his lifetime, he diffused knowledge into the community so that it could benefit him after he dies. So in essence, *Īsāl Sawāb* does not negate this verse, but in fact supports it. A man truly does not earn except what he strives for. In fact, just by virtue of a person becoming a part of the Muslim Ummah warrants him the right to be the recipient of the supplications and rewards of his fellow Muslim brothers.

Chapter Ten

Bid'a

10.1. The meaning of *Bid'a*.

Literal meaning:

Literally, *Bid'a* means to initiate or create something upon an unprecedented example.[216] One of the names of Allāh Almighty is *Badi'* (2:117).[217] This refers to how Allāh created everything in the skies and earth without a previous example to follow.

The meaning of *Bid'a* in Islamic Sharī'ah:

Imām al-Hararī writes:

وشرعا المحدث الذي لم ينص عليه القران و لا الحديث

'In Islamic Sharī'ah, *Bid'a* is a new matter for which there is no textual proof from the Qur'ān or Hadīth.'[218]

---

216 p. 415. *al-Sharh al-Qawīm fī Hall Alfāz al-Sirāt al-Mustaqīm*. Abd Allāh al-Hararī.
217 This word comes from the same root word as *Bid'a*.
218 p. 415. *al-Sharh al-Qawīm fī Hall Alfāz al-Sirāt al-Mustaqīm*. Abd Allāh al-Hararī.

10.2. The Prophet's guidance on Bid'a.

Repeatedly, the Prophet ﷺ warned his followers to refrain from innovative practices in Islamic Sharī'ah. As the final Prophet, he left a perfect role model for us to follow and he urged his followers not to initiate new matters. We must not change the number of Rak'āts in Salāh or alter when Hajj is performed.

Imām Nasā'ī reports in his *Sunan* from Jābir that the Prophet ﷺ said:

> 'The most truthful of dialogue is the dialogue of Allāh and the best of all guidance is the guidance of Muhammad. The worst matters are the new ones (*Muhdathāt*) and every *Muhdathāt* is *Bid'a*. Every *Bid'a* is misguidance and every misguidance is destined to the fire.'[219]

10.3. Did the Prophet declare all innovations as misguidance?

The above Hadīth seemingly suggests that the the Prophet ﷺ declared all *Bid'a* as misguidance. However, the classical scholars have divided *Bid'a* into different types. What justification exists to categorise *Bid'a* into different types?

In reality, the Prophet ﷺ did not declare *all Bid'a* as misguidance. Several Ahādīth of his confirm this;

a. The Mother of the Faithful Ā'isha (may Allāh be pleased with her) reports that the Prophet ﷺ said:

---

219 *Sunan Nasa'ī*. Book of the Two Eids. Chapter, the Sermon. Hadīth no, 1560. Similar reports are to be found in *Sahīh Muslim* (Hadīth no. 1435), *Sunan Ibn Māja* (Hadīth no. 44), *Sunan al-Dārmī* (Hadīth no. 208) and *Musnad Ahmad* (Hadīth no. 13815).

من احدث في امرنا هذا ما ليس منه فهو رد

> 'Whoever innovates [something] *which is not from our matter* [of Islām] then it is rejected.'[220]

What this saying clearly indicates is that not all *Bid'a* is rejected; rather, only those innovated practices which are alien to Islām are rejected.

b. Imām Muslim narrates a Hadīth through the chain of Jarīr ibn Abd Allāh, who reports that the Prophet ﷺ said:

> 'Whoever initiates a good practice in Islām then he will attain the reward for it and the reward of whoever acts upon it thereafter, without any shortcomings. And whoever initiates an evil practice, then he will carry the burden as well as the burden of whoever acts upon it thereafter, without any shortcomings.'[221]

What this Hadīth thus shows is that not *all* innovation is contrary to Islām. If this was the case, then the Prophet ﷺ would not have promised a reward for those who initiate a good practice.

c. Ibn Māja (d. 273/886) reports in his *Sunan* that the Prophet ﷺ said:

> '...and whoever initiates a *Bid'a* that Allāh and His Messenger are not pleased with, then upon him is the sin and the sin of whosoever acts upon it [thereafter]...'[222]

In clear terms, the Prophet ﷺ identified the abhorred *Bid'a* as the one which displeases Allāh and His Messenger.

---

220 *Sahīh al-Bukhārī.* Book of Sulah. Hadīth no. 2499.
221 *Sahīh Muslim.* Book of Knowledge. Hadīth no. 4830.
222 *Sunan Ibn Māja.* Introduction. 'Whoever revives a Sunna that has perished...' Hadīth no. 206.

d. The Qur'ān too implicitly suggests that not all innovated practices are wrong. Allāh states:

> '...and We sent Jesus, son of Maryam and gave him the *Injīl*. And We ordained in the hearts of those who followed him, compassion and mercy. But the priesthood they invented for themselves, We did not prescribe this for them, but they sought only to please Allāh. But they did not observe it with the right observance.' (57:27)

In this verse, the believers in the time of Jesus are praised as they were the people of 'mercy and kindness'. In addition to their ordained worship, they innovated the practice of priesthood (رهبانية). This involved refraining from certain permitted acts (like marriage) and gearing their entire energy towards worshipping their Lord.

Allāh or Jesus did not formally order priesthood. Despite this, Allāh affirmed this innovation and accepted it. Those who came after these believers were lamented, because they added *Shirk* to their worship and distorted the original message of Jesus. Al-Hararī writes:

> 'It is deduced from this verse that whoever innovates a practice which does not contravene the Sharī'ah, then this is not necessarily a misguided innovation. Rather, the agent is rewarded accordingly.'[223]

e. The scholars too have agreed that there are different types of *Bid'a*.

Imām Shāfi'ī declares:

> '*Bid'a* is of two types; *Bid'a Mahmūda* (praiseworthy innovation) and *Bid'a Mazmūma* (abhorred innovation). That

223 p. 418. *al-Sharh al-Qawīm fī Hall Alfāz al-Sirāt al-Mustaqīm*. Abd Allāh al-Hararī.

which complies with the Sunna is praiseworthy and that which opposes the Sunna is abhorred.'[224]

Imām Qurtubī (d. 671/1272) writes:

> 'Every *Bid'a* that originates from humans either has an origin in Islamic Sharī'ah or not. If it does have an origin, then it falls under the category of what Allāh has affirmed and what the Prophet encouraged. If the *Bid'a* contravenes what Allāh and His Prophet have ordered, then it is disliked and rejected.' [225]

On the Hadīth 'and every *Bid'a* is misguidance', Imām Qurtubī explains:

> '[With this saying] the Prophet ﷺ intended such matters which do not comply with the Qur'ān and Sunnah, or the actions of the Companions [and he did not mean all types of innovations unequivocally]. This is clear in his other saying 'Whoever initiates a good practice in Islām then he will attain the reward for it and the reward of whoever acts upon it thereafter, without any shortcomings. And whoever initiates an evil practice, then he will carry the burden as well as the burden of whoever acts upon it thereafter, without any shortcomings.' This is an indication that innovated practices can be disliked or can be praiseworthy.'[226]

Al-Hararī writes:

> 'The Hadīth 'and every *Bid'a* is misguidance' is categorised [in Usūl Fiqh terminology] as *al-Āmm al-Makhsūs*. In order words, the order is universal but specific to innovations that oppose

---

224 p. 11. *al-Islām Dīn al-Wastiyya wa al-I'tidāl*. Glossary for National Curriculum for Religious Teaching, Syria.

225 p. 87. Vol. I, part II. *Tafsīr al-Qurtubī*. Imām Qurtubī.

226 Ibid.

the Sharīʻah. If this Hadīth is not interpreted as such, then the Hadīth 'Whoever initiates a good practice in Islām...' will not make sense.' [227]

10.4. Other Categorisations of Bidʻa.

Imām al-Nawawī cites Sheikh Abū Muhammad Abd al-Azīz ibn Abd al-Salām, who categorised *Bidʻa* into the following types;

i. Compulsory:

This includes:

-The obligation to teach the sciences of the Arabic language.

-Studying secular sciences such as medicine and engineering.

ii. Forbidden:

For instance:

- Altering the way the Qur'ān is read.
- The Muslims who totally distort the name of Allāh in their *Zikr* sessions.[228]
- The beliefs of misguided Muslims such as the Qadariyyas, the Jabariyyas, Qādiānīs (Ahmadiyya) and so on. [229]

---

227 p 420. *al-Sharh al-Qawīm fī Hall Alfāz al-Sirāt al-Mustaqīm*. Abd Allāh al-Hararī.
228 p. 416. *al-Sharh al-Qawīm fī Hall Alfāz al-Sirāt al-Mustaqīm*. Abd Allāh al-Hararī
229 p. 12. *al-Islām Dīn al-Wastiyya wa al-I'tidāl*. Glossary for National Curriculum for Religious Teaching, Syria.

iii. Recommended:

This includes:

- The building of Mihrābs. The Mihrāb was first added to the Prophet's mosque at the end of the first century, in the time of Umar ibn Abd al-Azīz.[230]
- The building of schools and universities.
- The building of places for the Azān to be read.[231]
- Dotting the letters of the Qur'ān.[232]
- Celebrating the *Mawlid.* Al-Hararī writes that whoever thinks that the Mawlid is a misguided innovation is simply ignorant.[233]
- Writing صلي الله عليه و سلم after the Prophet's name is *Bid'a* as he himself did not do this. When he wrote a letter to Hirqal and Kisrā, he did not add these words.[234]

iv. Disliked:

This includes:

- The excessive decoration of mosques.
- According to Sheikh Ramadān Būtī, a leading scholar of Syria, a disliked *Bid'a* of recent times is the blaring of the name of the deceased over a microphone and asking people to pray for the deceased from the front car of a slow procession towards the

---

230 p. 417. *al-Sharh al-Qawīm fī Hall Alfāz al-Sirāt al-Mustaqīm*. Abd Allāh al-Hararī.
231 p. 417. Ibid.
232 Ibid.
233 Ibid.
234 p. 419. Ibid.

mosque or the cemetery.[235]

v. **Permissible:**

This concerns innovations that are morally neutral and are thus permitted, like putting different types of food on the table.[236]

10.5. Examples of innovations from the Companions.

- Abū Bakr ﷺ was the first to compile the Qur'ān in one document. This was not done in the time of the Prophet ﷺ.[237]

- Umar ﷺ famously began the practice of congregational Tarāwīh prayer. He commented: 'What a good innovation this is!' (نعمت البدعة هذه).[238]

- Umar ﷺ added a few words to the original *Talbiyya* of the Prophet ﷺ. He would recite:

  لبيك اللهم و سعديك الخير في يدك و العمل و الرغباء اليك

  No Companion objected to this addition because it complied and complemented the original words of the Prophet ﷺ.[239]

- Umar ﷺ moved the place of Maqām Ibrāhīm. In the time of the Prophet ﷺ and Abū Bakr, it was attached to the Ka'ba. Ibn Hajar (d. 852/1448) adds that none of the Companions opposed this action of Umar.[240]

---

235 p. 73. *Sunna Notes- Studies in Hadīth & Doctrine (Volume II; The Excellent Innovation in the Qur'ān and Hadīth.* Haddād, G.F.

236 p. 423. *al-Sharh al-Qawīm fī Hall Alfāz al-Sirāt al-Mustaqīm*. Abd Allāh al-Hararī.

237 p. 87. *Sunna Notes- Studies in Hadīth & Doctrine (Volume II; The Excellent Innovation in the Qur'ān and Hadīth.* Haddād, G.F.

238 p.92. Ibid.

239 p 419. *al-Sharh al-Qawīm fī Hall Alfāz al-Sirāt al-Mustaqīm*. Abd Allāh al-Hararī.

240 p. 88. *Sunna Notes- Studies in Hadīth & Doctrine (Volume II; The Excellent Innovation in the*

- Uthmān ﷺ added a second Azān for Friday prayers though this was not done in the time of the Prophet ﷺ. This practice is still in place today.[241]

- Khubaib ibn Addī initiated the practice of performing two Rak'ats Nafl before execution, as reported by al-Bukhārī in his *Sahīh*. [242]

- Bilāl ﷺ would perform two Rak'ats Nafl after every Wudū. The Prophet ﷺ told him this was the reason why he heard his footsteps in Paradise.[243]

10.6. 'All innovations are wrong' – the opinion of the Wahhābīs.

The classical and majority view in *Bid'a* contrasts with some Muslims who hold the view that all new practices in Islām are wrong. The Permanent Committee for Islamic Research and Legal Opinions (in Saudi Arabia) declared that:

> 'All innovations are deviations [from Islām], and there is no such thing as a good innovation.'[244]

Such an opinion does not explain why no Muslim objects to the teaching and studying of Arabic Grammar, Usūl Fiqh, Usūl Tafsīr and Usūl Hadīth.

Qur'ān and Hadīth. Haddād, G.F.

241 p 421. *al-Sharh al-Qawīm fī Hall Alfāz al-Sirāt al-Mustaqīm*. Abd Allāh al-Hararī.

242 *Sahīh al-Bukhārī*. Book of expeditions, Chapter, the Ghazwa of Raji', Hadīth no. 3777.

243 The Prophet (peace and blessings of Allāh be upon him) said to Bilāl at Fajr Prayer: 'Bilāl! Tell me about the deed for which you are most hopeful for reward in Islām, for, truly, I heard the sound of your sandals in Paradise.' He replied: 'I did not do anything for which I am more hopeful of reward except the fact I never perform Wudū in the day or night without praying what I must pray after such ablution.' The Prophet (peace and blessings of Allāh be upon him) said: 'With these two Rak'ats [you entered Paradise].' (*Sahīh al-Bukhārī*, Hadīth no. 1081) See p. 73. *Sunna Notes- Studies in Hadīth & Doctrine (Volume II; The Excellent Innovation in the Qur'ān and Hadīth*. Haddād, G.F.

244 p. 65. Cited in *The Response* (*Fix Your Deen* series). Translated by Dr. Richard Gauvain.

These are all innovations, because they were not done in the time of the Prophet or his Companions. They are classified as commendable innovations because they fall within the laws of Sharī'ah.

10.7. The refutation of the Wahhābīs.

10.7.1 'Commemorating Laila al-Isrā and Laila Nisf Sha'bān is *Bid'a*.'

- The Permanent Committee (3:59-61) declared:

> 'It is not permitted to celebrate any events other than the formal religious occasions that the law singles out [for celebration], namely the two Feasts (Eid al-Fitr & Eid al-Adhā). However, Mother's day, national days, birthdays, or times connected to other religious events, such as the Night Journey of the Prophet ﷺ [and the middle night of Sha'bān] or those dedicated to the opening of the mosque, should not be celebrated. For these kinds of celebrations are reprehensible innovations that are new to Islām and therefore invalid.'[245]

Answer:

It is *Mustahab* for Muslims to gather in the house of Allāh for the sake of His remembrance, propagating Islām and highlighting the flawless Sunna of the Prophet ﷺ. Abū Mūsā al-Asharī رضي الله عنه reports that the Prophet ﷺ said:

> 'Allāh Almighty descends on His creation on the middle night of Sha'bān and forgives His creation, except for the polytheist and

245 p. 71. Ibid.

the one who shows animosity.'[246]

Ā'isha (may Allāh be pleased with her) reports that the Prophet ﷺ spend the middle night of Sha'bān in extensive prayer to the extent she thought he had died. [247]

Regarding the night of mid-Sha'bān, Sheikh Ibn Taymiyya wrote:

> '[Some] said there is no difference between this night and other nights of the year. However, the opinion of many of the people of learning and that of the majority of our [Hanbalī] colleagues...is that it is a night of superior merit, and this is what is indicated by the words of Ahmad ibn Hanbal, in view of the many Ahādīth transmitted about it and in light of...the words and deeds transmitted from the early generations. Some of its merits have been narrated in the books of Hadīth...'[248]

10.7.2 'Reading Salām upon the Prophet ﷺ before Azān is *Bid'a.*'

Answer:

Urwa ibn Zubair ﷺ reports that a woman from Banū al-Najjār said:

> 'My house was the tallest house in relation to the mosque, and Bilāl would perform Fajr Azān upon it. He would come there at dawn time, sit and wait for Fajr time. When the time came for Azān, he would say: 'O Allāh! I praise you and seek your assistance on that Quraish establish Your religion.' She said:

---

246 *Musnad Ahmad.* Hadīth no. 6353.

247 Reported by al-Baihaqī and Tabarānī. Cited in *al-Islām Dīn al-Wastiyya wa al-I'tidāl.* Glossary for National Curriculum for Religious Teaching, Syria.

248 p. 208. *Sunna Notes- Studies in Hadīth & Doctrine (Volume II; The Excellent Innovation in the Qur'ān and Hadīth.* Haddād, G.F.

> 'Then he would perform the Azān. I swear by Allāh! I do not know of a single night when he did not read these words.'[249]

What this Hadīth explicitly shows is that performing a *Du'ā* before the Azān is the Sunna of the Muezzin of the Beloved Prophet, Bilāl ﷺ. Therefore, sending Salām upon the Prophet ﷺ, which too is a *Du'ā*, cannot be termed as a disliked innovation.

10.7.3. 'Salāh al-Tasbih is *Bid'a.*'

- The same Saudi scholars also reject Salāh al-Tasbīh:

> 'The *Tasābīh* prayers are a reprehensible innovation. The Hadīth which they are based upon is not reliable, hence these prayers should be rejected.'[250]

Answer:

Even if the Hadīth about Salāh al-Tasbīh is weak, then according to all the scholars, it is permissible to act upon a weak Hadīth in the area of encouraging virtuous acts (*Fazā'il al-A'māl*). But the scholars have found sufficient evidence to warrant its approval. Dr. Ahmad Īd writes that the validity of Salāh al-Tasbīh can be proven from the narrations of Abū Dāwūd, Ibn Māja, Ibn Khuzaima and al-Tabarānī. Imām Nawawī believes there is sufficient evidence to deem these prayers as recommended.[251] Therefore, referring to these prayers as innovation is incorrect.

---

249 *Sunan Abū Dāwūd*. Book of Salāh. Chapter, Azān on a Minaret. Hadīth no. 435.
250 p. 83. Cited in *The Response* (*Fix Your Deen* series). Translated by Dr. Richard Gauvain.
251 p. 83. Ibid.

10.7.4. 'The *Du'ā* after the obligatory Salāhs is *Bid'a*.'

Answer:

In the same way that the Prophet ﷺ did read Tarāwīh but not collectively, the Prophet ﷺ did perform Du'ā after Salāh but not collectively. Imām Muslim[252] reports from Thawbān that:

> 'When the Prophet ﷺ used to finish the Salāh, he would say *Astaghfirullāh* three times and say:
>
> اللهم انت السلام و منك السلام تبارکت ذا الجلال و الاكرام

Hence, the question is not whether the *Du'ā* after Salāh is forbidden or not as this is proven without doubt. As the example of Umar shows with Tarāwīh prayers, there is no harm in performing a religious duty collectively when it is proven the Prophet ﷺ did it individually. Moreover, doing it collectively will ensure that Muslims do not miss this perfect time to supplicate to Allāh. The Prophet ﷺ was asked about which *Du'ā* is most listened to. He replied: 'In the last part of the night and after the obligatory prayers.'[253]

10.7.5. 'Reading Salām upon the Prophet ﷺ loudly after the Azān is *Bid'a*.' [254]

Answer:

Countless Ahādīth stress the importance of the *Du'ā* and Salām upon the Prophet ﷺ after the Azān. The only difference is whether it should be read loudly or quietly. Most scholars do not oppose it being read loudly

252 *Sahīh Muslim*. Book of Mosques. Hadīth no. 931.
253 *Sunan al-Tirmidhī*. Hadīth no. 3421.
254 p. 101. *The Response* (*Fix Your Deen* series). Translated by Dr. Richard Gauvain.

because it can remind those Muslims who forget to recite it.[255]

10.7.6. 'Shaking hands after Salāh is *Bid'a.*'

- Sheikh Ibn Bāz writes in *Fatāwa Islāmiyya*:

> '[The practice of] shaking hands [with the person praying alongside you] after finishing Prayer (Salāh) is not Islamic in origin; it is, therefore a reprehensible innovation.'[256]

Answer:

The origin of shaking hands is Sunna. The fact that people have not always been observing this Sunna does not mean that it is no longer a recommended practice.

10.7.7. 'Collective *Zikr* is *Bid'a.*'

Answer:

Allāh says in the Qur'ān:

> 'And (O Muhammad) keep yourself patient with those who call to their Lord morning and afternoon, seeking His pleasure...' (18: 28)

> 'O believers! Remember Allāh excessively. And glorify His praises morning and afternoon.' (33: 41-2)

---

255 p. 23. *al-Islām Dīn al-Wastiyya wa al-I'tidal.* Glossary for National Curriculum for Religious Teaching, Syria. Sheikh Jibrīl Haddād writes that the practice of performing Salām upon the Prophet (peace and blessings of Allāh be upon him) after Azān loudly was introduced by Salāh al-Dīn Ayyūbī in Egypt and Shām (Syria, Lebanon, Palestine and Jordan).

256 p. 79. *The Response* (*Fix Your Deen* series). Translated by Dr. Richard Gauvain.

In both verses, Allāh has used the plural form. In other words, *everyone* must remember Allāh.

Abū Huraira reports that the Prophet ﷺ said:

> 'Verily for Allāh are appointed angels who circulate the streets seeking the people of *Zikr.* When they find a community remembering Allāh...they spread their wings to the earthly sky. Their Lord asks, though He knows better: 'What are My servants saying?' They reply: 'They are doing Your *Tasbīh,* Your *Takbīr,* Your *Hamd* and Your *Majd...*' [257]

This Hadīth is clear indication that collective *Zikr* is reported to Allāh and therefore not an act which contravenes Sharī'ah.

In the famous Hadīth Qudsī, Allāh says:

> 'And if My servant remembers Me in a gathering, I will remember him in a gathering much better than his.[258]

10.7.8. 'Saying the intention verbally before commencing Salāh is *Bid'a.*' [259]

Answer:

The Shāfi'ī scholars state that there is no harm in speaking one's intention aloud. In fact it is encouraged when (i) the person feels that the verbal uttering will help the heart (ii) the person feels he is vulnerable to the whispers (*Waswasa*) of the devil. [260]

---

257 *Sahīh al-Bukhārī.* Book of *Du'ās.* Chapter, the Superiority of the remembrance of Allāh. Hadīth no. 5929.
258 *Sahīh al-Bukhārī.* Book of Tawhīd. Hadīth no. 6856.
259 p. 84. *The Response* (*Fix Your Deen* series). Translated by Dr. Richard Gauvain.
260 pp. 84-5. *The Response* (*Fix Your Deen* series). Translated by Dr. Richard Gauvain.

10.7.9. 'Placing flowers on graves is Bid'a and an imitation of the infidels.'[261]

Answer:

Imām al-Bukhārī and Muslim report from Ibn Abbās ﷺ that:

> 'The Prophet ﷺ once passed by two graves and said: 'Both are being punished over trivial matters. As for one of them, he never took care when urinating. As for the other, he used to tell-tale.' The Prophet then asked for a wet plant which he snapped in half. He placed them on the graves and said: 'Perhaps their punishment will be lightened until the plant withers.'[262]

The branches of plants glorify Allāh as long as they are not dry. They bring Allāh's mercy to the deceased in the grave because, as with all living things, they praise Allāh. As for the claim that Muslims are imitating infidels, the Hadīth shows clearly that this is also the Sunna of the Prophet ﷺ. One can only be punished for imitating infidels if we set out intentionally to do so.

10.8. Conclusion.

In short, the worships ordained by the Prophet ﷺ are categorised into two types. The first are those worships which have been prescribed attached to a specific place, time, number and method. Such a type has to be performed exactly like the Prophet ﷺ performed it without addition or shortcomings. If someone does, then this falls under the Prophet's command that 'every *Bid'a* is misguidance.' Examples of such types of worship are the number of Rak'ats in the prescribed Salāhs, the fasting

261 p. 124. Ibid.
262 *Sahīh al-Bukhārī.* Book of Wudū, Chapter, what has been mentioned about urinating. Hadīth no. 211.

in Ramadān, the rituals of Hajj and the amount and recipients of Zakāh.

The second type are those worships which form general guidance to the Muslims and are not specific to a particular time, place, number or method. Muslims are free to perform these types of worship with more freedom. Examples are like Nafl prayers, Zikr, the recitation of the Qur'ān, *Du'ā* and Salām upon the Prophet ﷺ.[263]

It seems that the Wahhābīs have failed to acknowledge this important difference and simply use the criteria that if the Prophet did not do it in that exact manner, it is forbidden, wrong and reprehensible. This position defies common sense. The jurists are clear in stating that in Islamic Sharī'ah, everything is permissible until proven otherwise (الأصل في الأشياء الاباحة).[264] We are allowed to perform *Du'ā* whenever we want, unless Sharī'ah has stated otherwise, like when in the toilet. We are free to perform optional prayers freely, unless Sharī'ah has guided us otherwise, like at the time of Zawāl. This is why the Prophet ﷺ did not forbid Bilāl from the Nafls he performed after every ablution.

263 pp. 11-12. *al-Islām Din al-Wastiyya wa al-I'tidal.* Glossary for National Curriculum for Religious Teaching, Syria.

264 This is the principle which the majority of the Usūl Fiqh scholars adhere to. Support for this maxim is found in the Qur'ān. Allāh states that: 'He has explained to you in detail what is forbidden to you.' (6: 119). In other words, everything is permissible and if it is not, then the Qur'ān and Sunna have clearly defined it as forbidden. For more discussion on this, please refer to pp. 254-267, *Ma'ārif al-Ahkām.* Mufti Muhammad Khan Qadiri. Alami Da'wat Islamiyya Publications, Lahore.

Bibliography

The Holy Qur'ān.

A Commentary of Sūrah Fātiha based on Tibyān al-Qur'ān. Allāma Ghulām Rasūl Sa'idī. Translated by Ather Hussain al-Azhari, HSBT Publications, Birmingham, UK, 2009.

An Interview with the Qur'ān. Muhammad Rafīq Choudary. Markazī Maktaba Islāmī, Delhi, India, 1980.

Al-Aqīda al-Hasana (al-Mar'ūf bi) Aqā'id al-Islām. Hazrat Shāh Walī Allāh Muhaddith Delhvī. Edited by Moulāna Muftī Muhammad Khalīl Khān, Farīd Book Stall, Lahore, Pakistan, 1980.

Al-Aqīdah al-Tahāwiyya, Sharh wa Ta'līq. Muhammad Nāsir al-Dīn Albānī. Maktaba al-Ma'ārif li al-Nashr wa al-Tawdīh, Riyadh, Saudi Arabia, 2001.

Blessings & Salutations on the Best of Creation. Muhammad Nawaz Siddiqui Hazarvi. Faizan-Madinah Publications, Peterborough, UK, 2007.

Christians and Muslims from Double Standards to Mutual Understanding. H. Goddard. Curzon Press, Surrey, UK, 1995.

Darāsāt fī al-Tabshīr wa al-Istishrāq. Professor Abd al-Qādir Sayyid Abd al-Raūf. Usūl al-Dīn, al-Azhar University, Cairo, Egypt.

Al-Durar al-Sanniya fī al-Radd alā al-Wahhābiyya. Sayyid Ahmad ibn al-Sayyid Zainī Dahlān. Dār Jawā'mi al-Kilam Publications, Cairo, Egypt, 1991.

Ihyā Ulūm al-Dīn. Imām al-Ghazālī (d. 505/1111). Dār al-Fajr li al-Turāth, Cairo, Egypt, 1999.

Islam: The Basic Articles of Faith, according to the Beliefs of the Ahl Sunna wa al-Jama'a; A Modern English Translation of Bahar-e-Shariat. Part One. Crescent Publishing, Rochdale, UK, 1998.

Islām Dīn al-Wastiyya wa al-I'tidāl (Glossary for National Curriculum for Religious Teaching) Religious Endowment Department, Syria.

Al-Isrā wa al-Mi'rāj. Dr. Abd al-Halīm Mahmūd. 9th edition. Dār al-Ma'ārif, Cairo, Egypt.

Kanzul Imān. Maulāna Shāh Ahmad Razā Khān. English translation by Professor Shāh Farīd al-Haque. World Islamic Mission Pakistan, Karachi, Pakistan.

Al-Khasā'is al-Nabawiyya al-Kubrā. Jalāl al-Dīn al-Suyūtī (d. 911/1505). Al-Maktaba al-Qayyima, Cairo, Egypt.

La Nabiyya Ba'dī. Sahibzāda Sayyid Muhammad Amīn Ali Shāh. Bāb al-Hudā, Faisalabad, Pakistan, 1988.

Lisān al-Arab. Allāma Jamāl al-Dīn Muhammad ibn Mukarram Ibn Manzūr (d. 711/1311). Dār Ihyā al-Turāth al-Arabī Publications, Beirut, Lebanon, 1988.

Al-Maqāsid al-Hasana. Shams al-Dīn Muhammad ibn Abd al-Rahmān al-Sakhāwī (d. 902/1496). Dār al-Kutub al-Ilmiyya, Beirut, Lebanon, 2003.

Muhammad's Mecca in Religion in pre-Islamic Arabia. W.M. Watt. Edinburgh University Press, UK, 1998.

Al-Muntakhabāt al-Imdādiyya. M.I.H. Pirzada. Minta's Printers, Nottingham, UK, 1993.

'Provenance and Transmission' in The Koran, Critical concepts in Islamic Studies. Theodore Noldeke. Edited by Colin Turner. Routledge, Curzon, UK, 2004.

Al-Radd alā Mustafā Mahmūd fī Inkār al-Shafā'a. Abd al-Muhdī ibn Abd al-Qādir ibn Abd al-Hādī. Dār al-I'tisām, Cairo, Egypt, 1999.

Reflections: A Quest for Answers to Today's Questions. M.I.H. Pirzada. Al-Karam Publications, UK, 2009.

Sharh al-Aqā'id al-Nasfiyya. Allāma Sa'd al-Dīn al-Taftazānī (d. 793/1390). Maktaba Khair Kathīr, Karachi, Pakistan.

Sharh al-Aqīdah al-Wāsita li Sheikh al-Islām Ibn Taymiyya. Commentary by Muhammad ibn Sālih al-Athīmain. Maktaba al-Hikam al-Dīniyya, 2007.

Sharh al-Risāla al-Nāfi'a wa al-Hujaj al-Qāti'a. Sheikh Muhammad Abd al-Latīf Sālih al-Farfūr (d. 1407/1986). Dār al-Nu'mān li al-Ulūm

Publications, Damascus. Syria.

Al-Sharh al-Qawīm fī Hall Alfāz al-Sirāt al-Mustaqīm. Abd Allāh al-Hararī. Dar al-Mashā'ri, Beirut, Lebanon, 2004.

Al-Shifā. Abū al-Fadl Qādī Iyād ibn Mūsā ibn Iyād (d. 544/1149). Dār Ibn Hazam, Beirut, Lebanon, 2002.

Sirat Ahl as-Sunnah. Published by Sirat al-Muslimun, Manchester, UK, 2002.

Sunna Notes- Studies in Hadīth & Doctrine (Volume II; The Excellent Innovation in the Qur'ān and Hadīth.) Gibrīl. F. Haddād. Aqsa Publications, UK, 1995.

Tabarruk al-Sahāba bi Āthār Rasūl Allāh. Sheikh Muhammad Tāhir ibn Abd al-Qādir ibn Mahmūd al-Kurdī. Maktaba al-Qāhira Publications, Cairo, 1997.

Tahzīb al-Tahzīb. Hāfiz Shihāb al-Dīn Ahmad ibn Alī ibn Hajar al-Asqalānī (d. 852/1448). Dār Ihyā al-Turāth al-Arabī, 2nd edition, Beirut, Lebanon, 1993.

Tafsīr al-Qurtubī (Al-Jāmi li Ahkām al-Qur'ān). Allāma Abū Abd Allāh Muhammad ibn Ahmad al-Qurtubī (d. 671/1272). Dār al-Kutub al-Ilmiyya, Beirut, Lebanon, 2004.

Tashīh al-Aqā'id. Muhammad Abd al-Hāmid Budāyūnī. Ziā al-Qur'ān Publications, Lahore, Pakistan.

The Creed of Imām al-Tahāwī. Translated, Introduced and Annotated by Hamza Yusuf. Zaytuna Institute, USA, 2007.

The Obliteration of Falsehood (Jā al-Haqq). Muftī Ahmad Yār Khān. English Translation by Moulana Omar Dawood Qadri. Maktab Qadria, Bolton, UK, 2008.

The Oral Tradition of Classical Arabic Poetry. Michael Zwettler. Ohio State Press, USA, 1978.

The Response (***Fix Your Deen*** series). Translated by Dr. Richard Gauvain, 2009.

The Two Faces of Islām: The House of Sa'ud from Tradition to Terror. Stephen Schwarz. Doubleday, New York, USA, 2002.

Al-Usūl al-Thalātha. Muhammad ibn Abd al-Wahhāb (d. 1207/1792). Dār Taiba Publications, Riyadh, Saudi Arabia.

Ziā al-Qur'ān. Ziā al-Ummah Pīr Muhammad Karam Shāh al-Azharī (d. 1418/1998). Ziā al-Qur'ān Publications, Lahore, Pakistan, 1995.